COOKING DINNER

Simple Italian Family Recipes
Everyone Can Make

CLAUDIA PRUETT   RIMA BARKETT

Photographs by MICHAEL COLLOPY

MEGA
PRODUCTIONS
MADDEN ENTERTAINMENT GROUP ARTISTS

TO ANTHONY AND YASMIN

TO GREG, GREGORY, CRISTINA AND SOPHIA

Copyright ©2008 by A Tavola Together
Photographs copyright ©2008 by Michael Collopy

Printed in China by Island Heritage Publishing.
www.islandheritage.com

Published by MEG
94-411 Koaki Street, Waipahu, Hawaii 96797
Tel: (808) 564-8800 Fax: (808) 564-8877

Library of Congress Cataloging-in-Publication Data
Barkett, Rima and Pruett, Claudia
Cooking Dinner – Simple Italian Family Recipes Everyone Can Make
By Rima Barkett and Claudia Pruett, photographs by Michael Collopy – 1st ed.
2008911598   2008

ISBN   978-1-59700-778-8

We created **Cooking Dinner** because the habit of cooking and eating dinner together is disappearing from the daily routines of many American families. Since we have benefitted from our Italian heritage in preparing and sharing regular family meals, we want to celebrate its importance by demonstrating healthy meals are not a thing of the past, but rather, essential to strong, loving families. We believe that cooking and eating together is a pillar of family well-being. We are busy moms who cook with real families. We know that life in general is busy! So this book is for moms, dads and kids of all ages who want simple, stress-free cooking ideas, who like to eat good, home-made food, and who cherish quality family time. As a supplement to this cookbook, please visit our website *ATavolaTogether.com* for more recipes, weekly menus, shopping lists, kitchen secrets and a special "Kids Can Cook 2" section.

"You Should Open A Restaurant!"

I have always loved feeding people. Several times a week I would have friends over for dinner and many of them would say, "Rima, why don't you open a restaurant? There is such a need for your simple but great Italian food in our town." After years of hearing this, I decided to give it a try. My daughter, Yasmin, was in school full time and I was looking for something meaningful to do with my life. So I opened Café Luna Spaghetteria, an 80-seat restaurant.

My idea was to be open only for lunch and only on the days that Yasmin had school. What I did not know is that you cannot have a restaurant for a "hobby." A successful restaurant requires unbelievable effort and can "take over your life." I had no restaurant experience. None, not as a waitress, not as a manager, nada. I was the cook and my wonderful girlfriends were the waitresses. During the first month, I did not charge my customers since I needed to work out proportions and menu ideas. Even though my friends were a tremendous help, I realized I had to hire a professional staff.

A while after I opened Café Luna I needed a break. So I asked Claudia, who is the only person that I knew that loved to feed people great food as much as I did, if she would be a guest chef. Her love of cooking and feeding people made it easy for her to accept. For her it was like having a restaurant without the hassle, and for me it was time to get a little relief. Some clients would come on Wednesdays, Claudia's day, because they loved her food so much. As I said, this idea was born as a hobby. I still wanted to spend summers in Italy with my family. Claudia agreed to run the restaurant while I was gone, so I did not have to break this tradition.

After four amazing years, it came time to sell the restaurant. Many customers were sad but the new owners promised to learn my recipes. Claudia and I, excited about continuing our cooking partnership, decided to take new adventures by writing cookbooks and teaching kids how to cook through our A Tavola Together Foundation.

–Rima Barkett

Contents

30   46   60

Recipe List

90   138   178   200

The Power of Dinner

The power of dinner is incredible. Restoring this endangered tradition is essential. The magic created at the kitchen table forms a protective shield for all family members. We believe that great meals begin in the kitchen, are enjoyed at the family table and connect the family forever.

Cooking and eating together

Preparing a meal together is an educational and entertaining experience. Eating a meal together is a rewarding and nurturing event that strengthens the family bond. Sharing customs and values gives children a strong sense of family identity. It gives them a solid foundation for discovering their own place in the world. Studies show that mealtimes matter. A family dinner provides a safe forum for families to talk and share, promotes healthy eating habits, reduces the risks of substance abuse in teens, encourages positive attitudes and high academic achievement, and children overall are less inclined to submit to negative influences they encounter in society.

Cooking for your families takes time and effort. Sometimes, it can even be stressful, but the long-term benefits are priceless. Children who help prepare meals learn life-long cooking skills. Very young children love to play with pots and wooden spoons, the older ones enjoy helping parents cook, and teens appreciate the neutral environment of the kitchen. Home cooking allows you to control the quality of ingredients and teach your children about the importance of wholesome food choices. The comforting and satisfying aromas from simmering sauces and freshly-baked treats are beyond compare!

Four hands are better than two

Kids ages 8 to 12, if taught gradually, can be very helpful in the kitchen. The first rule is to never leave children in the kitchen unattended. If supervised, they can learn how to safely use a knife, the oven, stove and the mixer.

If making a new recipe, it is important to teach them to always read the ingredients list and directions before starting. Help them get all ingredients, help them measure and mix, and soon they can start making simple recipes like dressings and marinades on their own.

Kids 13 and over should be able to make all the recipes in this book.

Cooking takes practice but mostly love and patience. Do not let them get discouraged if the first attempts do not turn out as expected. A little encouragement goes a long way.

5

Easy Steps that Protect Family Well-Being

Choose a weekly menu and tear out the pre-made shopping list

The key to successful and stress-free cooking is having a weekly plan and a shopping list. Each weekly menu uses some ingredients more than once. Read through all the recipes for the week and prepare some ingredients in advance.

Buy all the groceries you need for the week, in one hour or less

Go to the store with your list. Know in advance what you need, this will save you time and money. You will not be tempted to buy excessive items and you will feel confident and prepared when it comes to making a delicious dinner.

Prepare the easy and delicious recipes

Frequently ask your kids – no matter what age – to help you. Follow our "Helping Hands" tips for ways to include younger children. Encourage older ones to make the recipes with just a little of your help. Or you can split the tasks – have your children prepare one aspect of the meal while you work on another. This will save you time and the kids will quickly learn basic cooking skills and become comfortable in any kitchen. Children who help prepare meals look forward to serving and eating them – even the picky eaters! They take pride in their cooking success, feel included in family time and are more eager to try a variety of foods.

Apply the "No-Excuse Rule"

Be consistent about family dinner nights. Resist the temptation to bargain by setting firm boundaries on what you are serving and at what time. There is no substitute for family dinner time!

Sit at the table and eat together

About five to ten minutes before dinner is ready, ask family members who are not already helping to set the table, dress the salad or toss the pasta. Now they are in the kitchen and will be more inclined to sit down and eat. At the table, keep conversations positive and non-confrontational. Encourage picky eaters to try at least one small bite of a food they don't like. After they taste it, if they don't want to keep eating it, they can say "no thank-you." Young kids need to try the same food several times before they become accustomed to eating it.

And…please turn off the TV.

The Organized Kitchen

The right equipment makes cooking easier and pleasurable. You do not need an expensive set of cookware or high-tech utensils to prepare excellent meals. However, it helps to have good-quality pieces. Purchase the best that you can afford and you will discover more satisfaction in cooking.

The bare necessities

COOKWARE: Pots and pans are available in a variety of materials. To take advantage of the superior heat-conducting abilities of copper with easy-care stainless steel, choose ones that are layered with a stainless steel cooking surface, a thick core of copper/aluminum and a stainless steel exterior. Look for riveted stainless steel handles and tight-fitting lids. Thick-bottomed, heavy-gauge and nonreactive cookware heat evenly, cook thoroughly and will not transfer "off" flavors to food.

BAKEWARE: Whether it's a well-used cookie sheet or a simple muffin pan, certain pieces will become your favorite baking partners. Heavy-duty cookie sheets and cake pans provide even heating for baked goods. Silicone liners are non-stick and reusable. Non-reactive glass or ceramic bakers are good choices for dishes such as lasagna, vegetable gratins and casseroles.

ELECTRICS: Small appliances are great helpers in the kitchen — saving time by speeding up food preparation. Blenders, food processors and mixers help create delicious creamed soups and sauces, fresh breads, fantastic cookies and delectable cakes in half the time and without the upper arm workout.

KNIVES: Good knives are indispensable in the kitchen. High-quality knives should feel balanced and have sufficient weight to facilitate chopping. Choose ones made from high-carbon stainless steel with blades that extend the full length and width of the handle.

TOOLS: Whisks, spoons and spatulas are tools that we just can't live without — playing the starring role in everyday cooking tasks. Other seldom-used gadgets hide in the back of a kitchen drawer waiting to be used a few times a year for special-occasion cooking. Keep your favorite tools organized and within reach.

OUTFITTING THE KITCHEN

Cookware

- ☐ double boiler
- ☐ roasting pan, large
- ☐ saucepans: small, medium and large
- ☐ sauté pan, large
- ☐ skillets: nonstick small and large
- ☐ stock pot, 4 to 6-quart
- ☐ tea kettle

Bakeware

- ☐ 2 baking sheets, rimmed
- ☐ 2 baking liners, silicone
- ☐ 1 bundt pan, 8 to 10-cup
- ☐ 1 loaf pan, 4 x 8-inch
- ☐ 1 muffin pan, 6 or 12-count
- ☐ 2 round cake pans, 8 or 9-inch
- ☐ 1 rectangle pan, 9 x 13-inch
- ☐ 1 square pan, 9 x 9-inch
- ☐ 2 wire cooling racks

Electrics

- ☐ blender: standard or immersion
- ☐ coffee maker
- ☐ food processor
- ☐ hand-held mixer, or stand mixer with beaters, paddle and dough hook
- ☐ toaster

Knives

- ☐ chef's knife
- ☐ paring knife
- ☐ serrated bread knife
- ☐ sharpening steel
- ☐ slicing knife

Tools

- ☐ bowls for mixing and prep: small, medium and large
- ☐ box grater
- ☐ can opener
- ☐ carving fork
- ☐ colander
- ☐ garlic press
- ☐ ladles: small and large
- ☐ measuring cups: liquid and dry
- ☐ measuring spoons
- ☐ meat tenderizer
- ☐ pasta server
- ☐ peppermill
- ☐ sieve/strainer
- ☐ silicone scrapers
- ☐ spatulas: metal and silicone
- ☐ spoons: serving, slotted and wooden
- ☐ tongs
- ☐ vegetable peeler
- ☐ wire whisk

Miscellaneous

- ☐ baster
- ☐ cake/pie server
- ☐ cake stand
- ☐ cheese board
- ☐ cheese grater
- ☐ cookie jar
- ☐ corkscrew
- ☐ cutting boards
- ☐ de-greasing cup
- ☐ fondue forks
- ☐ fondue pot
- ☐ funnel
- ☐ ice-cream scoop
- ☐ instant-read thermometer
- ☐ kitchen scale
- ☐ kitchen shears
- ☐ kitchen timer
- ☐ Mandoline
- ☐ melon ball scoop
- ☐ pasta pentola
- ☐ pastry brush
- ☐ pizza wheel (pizza cutter)
- ☐ pot holders
- ☐ potato masher
- ☐ potato ricer
- ☐ rolling pin
- ☐ salad spinner/dryer
- ☐ sifter
- ☐ zester for citrus

The Well-Stocked Pantry

Having a variety of ingredients on hand makes cooking possible anytime. Our friends are often surprised how we can make dinner so quickly, even at the last minute. We know the secret is to have a few basic ingredients at home and a few good recipes to choose from.

Herbs and spices

A bouquet of fragrant basil, a bunch of fresh parsley or sage and fresh-picked rosemary are some basic herbs found in our kitchens. They contribute important flavors and aromas to cooking. For best results, use fresh herbs when possible.

Spices have been used for centuries for their unique flavors and medicinal qualities. Salt and pepper are the most universal. Sea salt is obtained by evaporating seawater and has a "sweeter" flavor than table salt, which is pure sodium chloride. We suggest using sea salt in most recipes. Freshly ground black pepper is one of the most common spices in European cuisine. Black peppercorns are the most familiar, but red, green and white ones impart slight taste differences that are worth trying.

In the fridge

Refrigerator temperature has to be 38-40°F. Any higher than this is considered a "danger zone." At danger zone temperatures, bacteria grow rapidly in perishable foods such as meat, poultry, fish, milk and eggs.

Follow these simple suggestions to make sure your foods stay fresh, flavorful and safe:

- Divide large amounts of hot food into small containers (no more than 3″ deep) before putting them in the fridge. Large batches of hot food will not chill fast enough to remain safe.
- Foods should be refrigerated within 1 hour to help prevent bacteria growth.
- Store foods in well-sealed containers or resealable plastic bags.
- Allow room between containers so cold air can circulate evenly.
- If the electricity goes off, do not open the fridge or freezer door.
- If raw food has leaked in the refrigerator or freezer, wash the area with hot soapy water and sanitize with chlorine bleach.

Never taste perishable food to determine if it is still good. The way that food smells or looks is not a reliable indicator of its safety. Harmful bacteria can multiply in food without causing an "off" smell or taste. Throw it out if you are not sure.

PANTRY ESSENTIALS

Dry Goods

- [ ] barley
- [ ] cereal
- [ ] crackers or pita chips
- [ ] lentils
- [ ] pasta: spaghetti, penne, bowtie, etc.
- [ ] small pasta for soups
- [ ] rice: Arborio, Basmati, and long grain white

Canned Goods

- [ ] broth: chicken, beef and vegetable
- [ ] cannellini beans
- [ ] garbanzo beans (chick peas)
- [ ] kidney beans
- [ ] corn
- [ ] fruit
- [ ] olives
- [ ] peas
- [ ] tomato paste
- [ ] tomato: sauce and diced
- [ ] tuna

Other

- [ ] dried fruit
- [ ] jelly or jam
- [ ] peanut butter
- [ ] canola oil
- [ ] olive oil, regular
- [ ] extra-virgin olive oil
- [ ] red wine vinegar
- [ ] balsamic vinegar
- [ ] coffee: regular and decaf
- [ ] tea
- [ ] aluminum foil
- [ ] plastic wrap
- [ ] resealable plastic bags
- [ ] plastic containers
- [ ] waxed paper
- [ ] parchment paper

Baking Goods

- [ ] all-purpose flour
- [ ] baking powder
- [ ] baking soda
- [ ] chocolate chips, semisweet
- [ ] cocoa powder
- [ ] cornstarch
- [ ] cream of tartar
- [ ] non-stick baking spray
- [ ] pure vanilla extract
- [ ] sugar: white, brown, and powdered
- [ ] yeast, active-dry

Dried Herbs

- [ ] basil
- [ ] bay leaves
- [ ] dill
- [ ] Italian seasoning
- [ ] rosemary
- [ ] oregano
- [ ] thyme
- [ ] marjoram

Spices

- [ ] chili powder
- [ ] cinnamon
- [ ] curry powder
- [ ] garlic salt
- [ ] ginger, ground
- [ ] nutmeg, ground
- [ ] onion powder
- [ ] paprika
- [ ] pepper: black and white
- [ ] red pepper flakes
- [ ] salt, plain and sea

Fresh Foods

- [ ] bread
- [ ] fruit, variety
- [ ] lemons
- [ ] potatoes
- [ ] tomatoes

Fridge

dairy:

- [ ] butter
- [ ] cheese: mozzarella, Parmesan, chunk and grated
- [ ] cream cheese
- [ ] cream, heavy whipping cream
- [ ] half and half
- [ ] eggs
- [ ] milk
- [ ] yogurt

produce:

- [ ] carrots
- [ ] celery
- [ ] garlic cloves
- [ ] lettuce
- [ ] onions
- [ ] rosemary, fresh

miscellaneous:

- [ ] anchovies
- [ ] breadcrumbs
- [ ] dry white wine
- [ ] ketchup
- [ ] mayonnaise
- [ ] mustard: yellow and Dijon
- [ ] nuts: almonds, pinenuts and walnuts
- [ ] olives
- [ ] sun-dried tomatoes, oil-packed

Freezer

- [ ] bagels
- [ ] beef, lean ground
- [ ] bread
- [ ] chicken breasts: boneless and skinless
- [ ] ice cream
- [ ] green beans
- [ ] mixed vegetables
- [ ] peas
- [ ] prawns
- [ ] spinach, chopped

Weekly Menus & Shopping Lists

These Weekly Menus feature tasty combinations of our family-approved recipes. Each one offers a solution to the "What to Cook for Dinner" question, includes vegetarian alternatives and corresponds to its own shopping list. Use the handy, tear-out shopping lists included at the end of the book, or make your own with our template on page 29.

How to Plan a Weekly Menu:

We usually plan a Weekly Menu that includes four meals. Even we do not cook seven nights a week! There is always pizza night, a leftover night or a "go out to eat" night.

THINK SEASONALLY: First, we think about what's in season. We like to use local seasonal ingredients for better, healthier results and because they are often cheaper. Nowadays it is hard to know what's in season because most fruits and vegetables are available year round. Visit your local farmer's market to discover what's growing in your area. It's a great experience for the whole family!

LOOK AT THE WEEK: Then, we plan balanced meals based on one main dish ingredient for each night: chicken, beef, seafood or vegetarian. Keeping in mind our family favorites, we generally include a vegetable or two and a starch with every meal. We try to think of how one ingredient could be used twice during the week to save shopping and cooking time. We often introduce new recipes to keep dinner time exciting and we add a dessert once or twice a week. Anything you make from scratch – even if it has butter, sugar and cream – always tastes better and is healthier than store-bought sweets.

MAKE A LIST AND CHECK IT TWICE: Finally, we make a shopping list including items for each recipe, extra fruits and vegetables, school lunch ingredients and pantry essentials that might be running low. Shopping lists make grocery shopping more efficient and cost-effective. We take our list with us to the store and avoid going when we are hungry so we don't buy unnecessary snacks. We even use our grocer's online shopping cart. Nothing beats shopping from home or office and having the groceries delivered! Visit our website *www.ATavolaTogether.com* for more weekly menus and shopping lists.

WEEK 1: MENU

Lemon Chicken Piccata, pg 162
Spaghetti al Pesto, pg 120
Sautéed Peas, pg 186

Salmon with Pesto, pg 152
Risotto, pg 108
Green Beans, pg 195

Grilled Chicken with Herbs, pg 171
Risotto Cakes, pg 109
Creamed Spinach, pg 187

Fettuccine with Peas, pg 136
Baked Vegetables, pg 184
Garden Salad, pg 83

Dessert of the week:
Chocolate Chip Cookies, pg 206

_____

_____

_____

_____

_____

_____

_____

_____

_____

_____

_____

_____

GROCERY LIST

WEEKLY Ingredients

PRODUCE
- ☐ 2 large tomatoes for baking
- ☐ 1 bunch radishes
- ☐ 1 head green leaf lettuce
- ☐ 3 pounds fresh spinach or 1 pound frozen
- ☐ 1 bell pepper
- ☐ 1 small eggplant
- ☐ 1 pound fresh or frozen green beans
- ☐ 1 small summer squash
- ☐ 1 small zucchini squash
- ☐ 1 red onion
- ☐ 2 onions
- ☐ 1 bunch flat-leaf parsley
- ☐ 5 oz fresh basil
- ☐ 2 lemons

PANTRY
- ☐ 3 15-oz cans chicken broth
- ☐ 1 pound fettuccine

MEAT/POULTRY/FISH
- ☐ 3 pounds chicken breast: boneless, skinless fillets
- ☐ 1 pound salmon fillets

DAIRY
- ☐ 4 oz blue cheese crumbles
- ☐ 4 oz mozzarella or fontina cheese

MISCELLANEOUS
- ☐ 2 10-oz packages frozen peas
- ☐ 1 jar capers
- ☐ 1 oz pine nuts

PANTRY ESSENTIALS
(to have on hand)

STAPLES
- ☐ balsamic vinegar
- ☐ extra-virgin olive oil
- ☐ olive oil
- ☐ sea salt, plain salt, pepper
- ☐ all-purpose flour
- ☐ Arborio rice
- ☐ kidney beans
- ☐ spaghetti

FRIDGE
- ☐ eggs
- ☐ milk
- ☐ butter
- ☐ heavy whipping cream
- ☐ Parmesan cheese, chunk and grated
- ☐ garlic cloves
- ☐ carrots
- ☐ breadcrumbs
- ☐ dry white wine
- ☐ sun-dried tomatoes, oil-packed

FRESH
- ☐ tomatoes

HERBS AND SPICES
- ☐ oregano, dried
- ☐ thyme, dried
- ☐ nutmeg, ground

ADDITIONAL
Ingredients for dessert

- ☐ sugar
- ☐ baking soda
- ☐ cream of tartar
- ☐ pure vanilla extract
- ☐ semisweet chocolate chips

Extra Items for Your Family: milk, eggs, bread, fruits, vegetables, etc.

Al tavola, non si invecchia mai.
(At the table, one does not grow old.)
~ITALIAN PROVERB~

WEEK 2: MENU

Arrosto, pg 140
Penne Arrabbiata, pg 92
Cannellini Beans with Sage, pg 196

Lamb Chops, pg 146
Potatoes Gratin, pg 183
Tomato, Cucumber & Red Onion Salad,
  pg 62

Chicken Pizzaiola, pg 144
Spaghetti Café Luna, pg 104
Mixed Greens, pg 74

Eggplant Parmigiana, pg 192
Bruschetta, pg 48

Dessert of the week:
Ricotta Berry Cheesecake, pg 218

_____

_____

_____

_____

_____

_____

_____

_____

_____

_____

_____

_____

GROCERY LIST

WEEKLY Ingredients

PRODUCE
- ☐ 2 large tomatoes for salad
- ☐ 6 roma tomatoes
- ☐ 5 oz mixed greens
- ☐ 2 lemons
- ☐ 2 large eggplants
- ☐ 1 cucumber
- ☐ 1 red onion
- ☐ 2 bunches fresh basil
- ☐ 1 bunch fresh sage
- ☐ 1 bunch fresh mint
- ☐ 2 pounds potatoes

PANTRY
- ☐ 4 15-oz cans plain tomato sauce
- ☐ 2 15-oz cans cannellini beans
- ☐ 1 pound spaghetti

MEAT/POULTRY/FISH
- ☐ 1 4 to 5 pound eye of round roast
- ☐ 8 4-oz lamb chops
- ☐ 1 pound chicken breast:
     boneless, skinless fillets

DAIRY
- ☐ 4 oz feta cheese, crumbled
- ☐ 3 8-ounce balls fresh mozzarella
- ☐ ½ pint heavy whipping cream

MISCELLANEOUS
- ☐ 1 baguette

PANTRY ESSENTIALS
(to have on hand)

STAPLES
- ☐ balsamic vinegar
- ☐ extra-virgin olive oil
- ☐ olive oil
- ☐ sea salt, plain salt, pepper
- ☐ canola oil or peanut oil
     for frying
- ☐ red wine vinegar
- ☐ all-purpose flour
- ☐ diced tomatoes, canned
- ☐ penne pasta
- ☐ chicken broth

FRIDGE
- ☐ eggs
- ☐ milk
- ☐ butter
- ☐ Parmesan cheese,
     chunk and grated
- ☐ onion
- ☐ garlic cloves

HERBS AND SPICES
- ☐ fresh rosemary
- ☐ red pepper flakes
- ☐ nutmeg, ground

ADDITIONAL
Ingredients for dessert
- ☐ sugar
- ☐ pure vanilla extract
- ☐ cornstarch
- ☐ 8 oz plain yogurt
- ☐ 16 oz ricotta cheese
- ☐ 1 pkg graham crackers
- ☐ 1 pint blueberries

Extra Items for Your Family: milk, eggs, bread, fruits, vegetables, etc.

There are 4 basic food groups:
milk chocolate, dark chocolate, white chocolate and chocolate truffles.
~AUTHOR UNKNOWN~

WEEK 3: MENU

Spaghetti al Ragu, pg 98
Spinach Frittata, pg 55
Focaccia, pg 32

Chicken Pinwheels, pg 166
Mashed Potatoes, pg 199
Carrots by Rose, pg 180

Lasagna, pg 94
Caprese Salad, pg 68

Farfalle Caprese, pg 134
Caesar Salad, pg 82

Dessert of the week:
Strawberry Tiramisu, pg 210

_____

_____

_____

_____

_____

_____

_____

_____

_____

_____

_____

_____

_____

_____

_____

_____

GROCERY LIST

WEEKLY Ingredients

PRODUCE
- ☐ 4 large tomatoes for salad
- ☐ 2 heads romaine lettuce
- ☐ 2 pounds carrots
- ☐ 3 pounds russet potatoes
- ☐ 2 onions
- ☐ 1 bunch fresh basil

PANTRY
- ☐ 2 15-oz cans plain tomato sauce
- ☐ 1 pound bowtie pasta
- ☐ 1 pound lasagna pasta

MEAT/POULTRY/FISH
- ☐ 1 pound lean ground beef
- ☐ 1 pound chicken breast: boneless, skinless fillets

DAIRY
- ☐ 2 8-ounce balls fresh mozzarella
- ☐ 1 dozen fresh eggs

MISCELLANEOUS
- ☐ 1 bag croutons
- ☐ 1 12-oz bottle club soda
- ☐ 2 10-oz pkgs frozen spinach, chopped

PANTRY ESSENTIALS
(to have on hand)

STAPLES
- ☐ extra-virgin olive oil
- ☐ olive oil
- ☐ sea salt, plain salt, pepper
- ☐ all-purpose flour
- ☐ cornstarch
- ☐ active dry yeast
- ☐ tomato paste
- ☐ spaghetti

FRIDGE
- ☐ eggs
- ☐ milk
- ☐ butter
- ☐ heavy whipping cream
- ☐ Parmesan cheese, chunk and grated
- ☐ mozzarella cheese
- ☐ garlic cloves
- ☐ Dijon mustard
- ☐ dry white wine
- ☐ anchovies

HERBS AND SPICES
- ☐ nutmeg, ground

ADDITIONAL
Ingredients for dessert
- ☐ sugar
- ☐ powdered sugar
- ☐ cognac
- ☐ 1 12-oz pkg Italian ladyfinger cookies
- ☐ 16 oz mascarpone cheese
- ☐ 16 oz frozen strawberries
- ☐ 1 pint fresh strawberries

Extra Items for Your Family: milk, eggs, bread, fruits, vegetables, etc.

An onion can make people cry,
but there has never been a vegetable invented to make them laugh.
~WILL ROGERS~

WEEK 4: MENU

Veal with Sherry, pg 164
White Rice, pg 137
Broccoli, pg 197

Penne con Scampi, pg 112
Garden Salad, pg 83

Spaghetti with Simple Tomato Sauce,
 pg 111
Peperonata, pg 198

Sea Bass in Parchment, pg 168
Basmati Rice, pg 137
Mixed Greens, pg 74

Dessert of the week:
Mocha Marble Cake, pg 204

_____
_____
_____
_____
_____
_____
_____
_____
_____
_____
_____
_____
_____
_____
_____
_____
_____
_____
_____
_____
_____

GROCERY LIST

WEEKLY Ingredients

PRODUCE
- ☐ 1 head green leaf lettuce
- ☐ 5 oz mixed greens
- ☐ 1 bunch radishes
- ☐ 3 bell peppers, red, yellow, green
- ☐ 1 pound fresh broccoli
- ☐ 1 small zucchini squash
- ☐ 8 oz white mushrooms
- ☐ 1 bunch flat-leaf parsley
- ☐ 1 bunch fresh oregano
- ☐ 1 bunch fresh thyme

PANTRY
- ☐ 1 bottle dry sherry
- ☐ 1 bottle brandy
- ☐ 1 pound spaghetti pasta
- ☐ 1 pound penne pasta

MEAT/POULTRY/FISH
- ☐ 1½ pounds sea bass fillets
- ☐ 1 pound medium prawns
- ☐ 1 pound veal scaloppine

DAIRY
- ☐ 4 oz blue cheese crumbles

PANTRY ESSENTIALS
(to have on hand)

STAPLES
- ☐ balsamic vinegar
- ☐ extra-virgin olive oil
- ☐ olive oil
- ☐ sea salt, plain salt, pepper
- ☐ all-purpose flour
- ☐ long grain white rice
- ☐ Basmati rice
- ☐ kidney beans
- ☐ plain tomato sauce
- ☐ diced tomatoes, canned
- ☐ parchment paper

FRIDGE
- ☐ eggs
- ☐ milk
- ☐ butter
- ☐ heavy whipping cream
- ☐ Parmesan cheese, chunk and grated
- ☐ onion
- ☐ garlic cloves
- ☐ carrots
- ☐ celery
- ☐ breadcrumbs

FRESH
- ☐ tomatoes
- ☐ potatoes
- ☐ lemon

HERBS AND SPICES
- ☐ red pepper flakes

ADDITIONAL
Ingredients for dessert
- ☐ sugar
- ☐ brown sugar
- ☐ powdered sugar
- ☐ baking soda
- ☐ baking powder
- ☐ coffee
- ☐ semisweet chocolate chips
- ☐ pure vanilla extract
- ☐ 1 cup sour cream

Extra Items for Your Family: milk, eggs, bread, fruits, vegetables, etc.

WEEK 5: MENU

Grilled Tri-tip, pg 174
Fettuccine Alfredo, pg 38
Roasted Asparagus, pg 188

Chicken Cacciatora, pg 142
Polenta, pg 107
Green Beans, pg 195

Tri-tip Salad, pg 88
Creamy Tomato Soup, pg 86
Focaccia, pg 32

Penne with Asparagus, pg 132
Mediterranean Salad, pg 36

Dessert of the week:
Cinnamon Pear Cake, pg 222

_____
_____
_____
_____
_____
_____
_____
_____
_____
_____
_____
_____
_____
_____
_____
_____
_____
_____
_____

GROCERY LIST

WEEKLY Ingredients

PRODUCE
- ☐ I head romaine lettuce
- ☐ 5 oz mixed greens
- ☐ 3 pounds fresh asparagus
- ☐ I pound fresh green beans
- ☐ I bunch fresh rosemary
- ☐ I bunch fresh thyme
- ☐ I bunch fresh basil
- ☐ I bunch flat leaf parsley
- ☐ I bunch fresh oregano

PANTRY
- ☐ I 16-oz pkg polenta/cornmeal
- ☐ 3 15-oz cans chicken broth
- ☐ I can black olives
- ☐ I 28-oz can, good quality, diced tomatoes
- ☐ I pound fresh fettuccine pasta

MEAT/POULTRY/FISH
- ☐ I pound chicken drumsticks
- ☐ I pound chicken thighs
- ☐ I 2-pound tri-tip roast

DAIRY
- ☐ 8 oz blue cheese crumbles
- ☐ I pint heavy whipping cream
- ☐ 4 oz feta cheese

MISCELLANEOUS
- ☐ I 12-oz bottle club soda
- ☐ 8 oz dried cranberries
- ☐ I bag potato chips

PANTRY ESSENTIALS
(to have on hand)

STAPLES
- ☐ balsamic vinegar
- ☐ extra-virgin olive oil
- ☐ olive oil
- ☐ sea salt, plain salt, pepper
- ☐ garlic salt
- ☐ all-purpose flour
- ☐ active dry yeast
- ☐ plain tomato sauce
- ☐ walnuts
- ☐ penne pasta

FRIDGE
- ☐ eggs
- ☐ milk
- ☐ butter
- ☐ heavy whipping cream
- ☐ Parmesan cheese, chunk and grated
- ☐ onion
- ☐ garlic cloves
- ☐ carrots
- ☐ celery
- ☐ Dijon mustard
- ☐ dry white wine
- ☐ sun-dried tomatoes, oil-packed

FRESH
- ☐ tomatoes
- ☐ lemon

HERBS AND SPICES
- ☐ nutmeg, ground

ADDITIONAL
Ingredients for dessert
- ☐ sugar
- ☐ brown sugar
- ☐ baking soda
- ☐ baking powder
- ☐ cinnamon
- ☐ ginger, ground
- ☐ nutmeg, ground
- ☐ pure vanilla extract
- ☐ ½ cup sour cream
- ☐ 2 large firm pears

Extra Items for Your Family: milk, eggs, bread, fruits, vegetables, etc.

WEEK 6: MENU

Grilled Chicken with Herbs, pg 171
Spaghetti Café Luna, pg 104
Sautéed Zucchini, pg 195

Ossobuco, pg 160
Risotto Milanese, pg 128
Sautéed Peas, pg 186

Almond Baked Halibut, pg 145
Roasted Potatoes, pg 189
Brussels Sprouts, pg 182

Penne al Forno, pg 126
Zucchini Frittata, pg 54
Caesar Salad, pg 82

Dessert of the week:
Double Chocolate Biscotti, pg 216

_____
_____
_____
_____
_____
_____
_____
_____
_____
_____
_____
_____
_____
_____
_____
_____
_____

GROCERY LIST

WEEKLY Ingredients

PRODUCE
- ☐ 2 heads romaine lettuce
- ☐ 1 pound brussels sprouts
- ☐ 8 to 10 medium zucchini squash
- ☐ 2 pounds new or red potatoes
- ☐ 4 pounds yellow onions
- ☐ 2 leeks
- ☐ 2 lemons
- ☐ 1 bunch flat leaf parsley

PANTRY
- ☐ 1 15-oz can beef broth
- ☐ 5 15-oz cans chicken broth

MEAT/POULTRY/FISH
- ☐ 1½ pounds halibut fillets
- ☐ 2 pounds veal shanks
- ☐ 1 pound chicken breast:
     boneless, skinless fillets

MISCELLANEOUS
- ☐ 1 bag croutons
- ☐ 2 10-oz packages frozen peas
- ☐ 1 envelope saffron
- ☐ 8 oz almond meal
     (finely ground almonds)

PANTRY ESSENTIALS
(to have on hand)

STAPLES
- ☐ balsamic vinegar
- ☐ extra-virgin olive oil
- ☐ olive oil
- ☐ sea salt, plain salt, pepper
- ☐ garlic salt
- ☐ all-purpose flour
- ☐ Arborio rice
- ☐ plain tomato sauce
- ☐ spaghetti
- ☐ penne

FRIDGE
- ☐ eggs
- ☐ milk
- ☐ butter
- ☐ heavy whipping cream
- ☐ Parmesan cheese,
     chunk and grated
- ☐ onion
- ☐ garlic cloves
- ☐ carrots
- ☐ celery
- ☐ Dijon mustard
- ☐ dry white wine
- ☐ anchovies
- ☐ breadcrumbs

HERBS AND SPICES
- ☐ oregano, dried
- ☐ thyme, dried
- ☐ nutmeg, ground

ADDITIONAL
Ingredients for dessert

- ☐ sugar
- ☐ brown sugar
- ☐ cocoa powder
- ☐ baking soda
- ☐ semisweet chocolate chips
- ☐ white chocolate chips
- ☐ pure vanilla extract
- ☐ 1 small jar Nutella
     (choc-hazelnut spread)

Extra Items for Your Family: milk, eggs, bread, fruits, vegetables, etc.

WEEK 7: MENU

Roast Chicken with Vegetables, pg 177
Garden Salad, pg 83

Fondue Chinoise, pg 156
French Fries, pg 190
Mixed Greens, pg 74

Scallops Marsala, pg 158
Basmati Rice, pg 137
Carrots by Rose, pg 180

Butternut Squash Soup, pg 66
Rice & Artichoke Torta, pg 53
Focaccia, pg 32

Dessert of the week:
Fruit Salad, pg 202

_____
_____
_____
_____
_____
_____
_____
_____
_____
_____
_____
_____
_____
_____
_____
_____

GROCERY LIST

WEEKLY Ingredients

PRODUCE
- ☐ 1 head green leaf lettuce
- ☐ 5 oz mixed greens
- ☐ 2 butternut squash
- ☐ 2 pounds carrots
- ☐ 2 large tomatoes for salad
- ☐ 3 pounds potatoes for frying
- ☐ 4 red potatoes
- ☐ 1 bunch fresh sage
- ☐ 1 bunch radishes
- ☐ 1 bunch flat leaf parsley
- ☐ 1 bunch fresh thyme
- ☐ 1 bunch fresh basil

PANTRY
- ☐ 1 15-oz jar mayonnaise
- ☐ 3 15-oz cans chicken broth
- ☐ 4 15-oz cans beef broth
- ☐ 1 6-oz jar marinated artichoke hearts
- ☐ 1 8-oz jar Béarnaise sauce
- ☐ 1 48-oz bottle canola oil for frying
- ☐ 1 bottle Marsala wine

MEAT/POULTRY/FISH
- ☐ 1 pound large scallops
- ☐ 2 pounds eye of round, thinly sliced
- ☐ 1 roasting chicken, 4 to 5 pounds

DAIRY
- ☐ 4 oz blue cheese crumbles
- ☐ 4 oz Asiago cheese

MISCELLANEOUS
- ☐ 2 10-oz packages frozen peas
- ☐ 1 Sterno for fondue pot (canned cooking fuel)
- ☐ 1 12-oz bottle club soda

PANTRY ESSENTIALS
(to have on hand)

STAPLES
- ☐ balsamic vinegar
- ☐ extra-virgin olive oil
- ☐ olive oil
- ☐ sea salt, plain salt, pepper
- ☐ all-purpose flour
- ☐ active dry yeast
- ☐ Basmati rice
- ☐ kidney beans

FRIDGE
- ☐ eggs
- ☐ butter
- ☐ heavy whipping cream
- ☐ Parmesan cheese, chunk and grated
- ☐ onion
- ☐ garlic cloves
- ☐ celery
- ☐ breadcrumbs
- ☐ ketchup
- ☐ dry white wine

FRESH
- ☐ tomatoes

HERBS AND SPICES
- ☐ curry powder
- ☐ ginger, ground
- ☐ rosemary, fresh

ADDITIONAL
Ingredients for dessert
- ☐ fresh fruit
- ☐ orange juice

Extra Items for Your Family: milk, eggs, bread, fruits, vegetables, etc.

WEEK 8: MENU

Chicken Roman Style, pg 176
Baked Gnocchi, pg 117
Garden Salad, pg 83

Spaghetti Carbonara, pg 124
Sautéed Peas, pg 186

Brasato with Red Wine, pg 148
Polenta, pg 107
Caramelized Cauliflower, pg 197

Minestrone, pg 78
Caesar Salad, pg 82

Dessert of the week:
Nonno's Polenta Cake, pg 214

_____

_____

_____

_____

_____

_____

_____

_____

_____

_____

_____

_____

_____

_____

GROCERY LIST

WEEKLY Ingredients

PRODUCE
- [ ] I head green leaf lettuce
- [ ] 2 heads romaine lettuce
- [ ] I bunch radishes
- [ ] 2 pounds carrots
- [ ] I stalk celery
- [ ] I head cauliflower
- [ ] I small cabbage
- [ ] 4 pounds baking potatoes
- [ ] I leek
- [ ] I zucchini squash
- [ ] I bunch fresh thyme
- [ ] I bunch fresh oregano
- [ ] ¼ pound green beans, fresh or frozen

PANTRY
- [ ] 2 15-oz cans plain tomato sauce
- [ ] 2 15-oz cans chicken broth
- [ ] I 16-oz pkg polenta/cornmeal

MEAT/POULTRY/FISH
- [ ] I 3-pound top sirloin roast
- [ ] 4 oz pancetta
- [ ] 2 pounds chicken thighs, boneless, skinless

DAIRY
- [ ] 8 oz blue cheese crumbles
- [ ] 4 oz fontina cheese
- [ ] 4 oz mozzarella cheese

MISCELLANEOUS
- [ ] I jar whole cloves
- [ ] 2 bottles good quality Cabernet
- [ ] 2 10-oz packages frozen peas
- [ ] I jar capers

PANTRY ESSENTIALS
(to have on hand)

STAPLES
- [ ] balsamic vinegar
- [ ] extra-virgin olive oil
- [ ] olive oil
- [ ] sea salt, plain salt, pepper
- [ ] cannellini beans
- [ ] kidney beans
- [ ] spaghetti
- [ ] small pasta for soup

FRIDGE
- [ ] eggs
- [ ] butter
- [ ] half and half
- [ ] heavy whipping cream
- [ ] Parmesan cheese, chunk and grated
- [ ] onions
- [ ] garlic cloves
- [ ] Dijon mustard
- [ ] dry white wine
- [ ] anchovies

FRESH
- [ ] tomatoes
- [ ] lemon

HERBS AND SPICES
- [ ] oregano, ground
- [ ] rosemary, fresh
- [ ] bay leaves

ADDITIONAL
Ingredients for dessert
- [ ] cake flour
- [ ] I box powdered sugar
- [ ] baking powder
- [ ] fresh berries

Extra Items for Your Family: milk, eggs, bread, fruits, vegetables, etc.

A good meal soothes the soul and revives the body

~AUTHOR UNKNOWN~

WEEKLY MENU

Menus:

_____
_____
_____
_____
_____
_____
_____
_____
_____
_____
_____
_____

Dessert of the week:

_____
_____
_____

ADDITIONAL
Ingredients for dessert

☐ _____
☐ _____
☐ _____
☐ _____

GROCERY LIST

WEEKLY Ingredients

PRODUCE

☐ _____
☐ _____
☐ _____
☐ _____
☐ _____
☐ _____
☐ _____

PANTRY

☐ _____
☐ _____
☐ _____
☐ _____
☐ _____
☐ _____
☐ _____

MEAT/POULTRY/FISH

☐ _____
☐ _____
☐ _____
☐ _____
☐ _____
☐ _____

DAIRY

☐ _____
☐ _____
☐ _____
☐ _____

MISCELLANEOUS

☐ _____
☐ _____
☐ _____
☐ _____

Extra Items for Your Family: milk, eggs, bread, fruits, vegetables, etc.

PANTRY ESSENTIALS
(to have on hand)

STAPLES

☐ _____
☐ _____
☐ _____
☐ _____
☐ _____
☐ _____
☐ _____
☐ _____
☐ _____

FRIDGE

☐ _____
☐ _____
☐ _____
☐ _____
☐ _____
☐ _____
☐ _____
☐ _____

FRESH

☐ _____
☐ _____
☐ _____
☐ _____
☐ _____
☐ _____

HERBS AND SPICES

☐ _____
☐ _____
☐ _____
☐ _____
☐ _____

family favorites

WE KNOW that for every one of us, the first priority in life is the well-being of our family. The magical benefits of routinely eating home-cooked meals together continue to protect our loved-ones even when we are apart.

Focaccia

PREP TIME: 5 MINUTES **RISING TIME:** 3 HOURS **COOK TIME:** 20 MINUTES **SERVES:** 16

When we first opened Café Luna Spaghetteria, we had a very hard time finding great bread. Our friend Elena, an Italian restaurateur, shared her secret for this incredibly easy and delicious focaccia. It quickly became a favorite of customers and friends. Children especially love to help make it and eat it. When Rima's daughter Yasmin helped at the restaurant, she would be in charge of spreading the dough in the pan. She always wore an apron, since it can be a little messy.

3 cups flour

1 tablespoon sea salt

1 tablespoon active dry yeast, about 1½ packages

1¼ cups club soda, or sparkling water

½ cup olive oil, not extra-virgin

DID YOU KNOW?

Rising time is important! Bread dough that has no added sugar needs to rise twice to allow the starch in the flour to break down into food for the yeast

HELPING HANDS

Children can spread the dough in the pan and make the dimples with their fingertips.

KITCHEN TIP:

DO NOT open the oven while the focaccia is baking! If you do, the heat will escape.

DAY BEFORE OR 2 HOURS AHEAD:

Pour flour into a large mixing bowl. Add salt and yeast. Stir to combine. Add club soda. Beat for 3 minutes with an electric mixer fitted with a dough hook attachment. Start on low then increase speed to high.

Or mix the dough with your hands until the flour has absorbed all the water and does not stick to the bowl but a little to your fingers.

Cover bowl with plastic wrap and let rise overnight at room temperature or in a warm place for 2 hours. An oven heated for just 2 minutes will do.

Pour olive oil onto a 9 x 12-inch baking sheet with 1-inch sides.

Transfer dough to pan and gently spread to fill pan. With your hands, put some of the oil that is at the bottom of the pan on top of the dough. Or flip it over so both sides are bathed in olive oil. Make little dimples on the top of the focaccia with your fingers. Let rise in a warm place for 1 hour.

Preheat oven to 450°F.

Make more dimples on the top of the dough. Bake focaccia for 20 to 25 minutes or until golden brown. Remove from oven and let stand for 10 minutes or until the oil is absorbed. Cut into squares or long slices and serve the same day.

VARIATIONS For a different flavor, add thinly sliced tomatoes, zucchini, onions or vegetables on top just before you bake it. A common Italian variation is to add fresh rosemary, sliced onions and sliced olives on top.

Mediterranean Salad

PREP TIME: 10 MINUTES **SERVES:** 4 TO 6

This is a delicious lunch or dinner salad combining savory Mediterranean flavors with the sweet taste of dried cranberries.

DID YOU KNOW?

Cranberries contain significant amounts of antioxidants and other phytonutrients that help protect against heart disease and cancer.

HELPING HANDS

Young children can help measure the salad ingredients and sprinkle them on the mixed greens.

FOR THE SALAD:

6 cups mixed greens, about 5 ounces, rinsed and dried

¼ cup dried cranberries

¼ cup sun-dried tomatoes, oil-packed, cut into small pieces

4 ounces feta cheese, crumbled

½ cup walnut halves, toasted

FOR THE DRESSING:

2 tablespoons balsamic vinegar

1 teaspoon Dijon mustard

½ teaspoon sugar

½ teaspoon sea salt

Dash freshly ground pepper

½ cup extra-virgin olive oil

Combine the vinegar, mustard, sugar, salt and pepper in a small bowl. While gently whisking, gradually add the olive oil until it is all thoroughly mixed.

Place greens, cranberries, sun-dried tomatoes and feta cheese in a large salad bowl. Toss with the dressing. Garnish with toasted walnuts.

Serve immediately.

KITCHEN TIP:

To toast walnuts, spread them evenly on a baking sheet and toast in a preheated 350°F oven for 8 to 10 minutes. Allow to cool before storing in an airtight container.

Fettuccine Alfredo

PREP TIME: 5 MINUTES   **COOK TIME:** 10 MINUTES   **SERVES:** 4 TO 6

Considered to be Italian all over the world – except in Italy – this creamy delight is based on the butter and cheese sauce created by a Roman restaurateur, Alfredo. He became famous across the ocean by catering to Americans. This is a very simple recipe, as long as you follow the directions exactly!

½ cup butter, 1 stick

½ cup grated Parmesan cheese (purchased from your market's deli or refrigerated section). Do not use freshly grated.

1 cup heavy whipping cream

1 pound fettuccine pasta, preferably fresh

½ cup freshly grated Parmesan cheese for garnish

CURIOSITY:
To an Italian, Alfredo is the name of a waiter, not a sauce.

HELPING HANDS
Young children can help measure the Parmesan cheese.

KITCHEN TIP:
This pasta has to be eaten hot! For best results, use warm plates to serve it, so it will stay creamy longer.

Bring 4 quarts of water to a boil in a large pot over high heat. When the water is boiling, add 2 tablespoons salt and fettuccine. Reduce heat to medium-high and cook uncovered, according to package directions, stirring occasionally.

Meanwhile, warm cream in a small saucepan over low heat. Remove from heat just before it boils.

Melt butter in a separate small saucepan over low heat. Do not let it brown! When melted, add grated Parmesan cheese and stir for 1 minute.

Add heated cream and simmer on low for 1 more minute, stirring constantly.

Meanwhile, pour hot water into a serving bowl and let stand. This is an important step which serves to warm the bowl.

When Alfredo sauce and fettuccine are ready, pour out the water and dry the serving bowl. Pour the sauce into the serving bowl, drain the cooked fettuccine, add to the bowl and toss with the sauce. Sprinkle with freshly grated Parmesan cheese. Serve immediately!

Chicken Cutlet Milanese

PREP TIME: 10 MINUTES **COOK TIME:** 10 MINUTES **SERVES:** 4

As a young girl, Claudia helped her Mom make dinner by pounding the chicken and soaking it in the egg mixture. She still makes these quick and easy chicken cutlets on busy nights.

1 pound boneless, skinless chicken breast fillets, pg 253

1 large egg

⅛ cup milk

½ teaspoon sea salt

Dash freshly ground pepper

1 cup bread crumbs

4 tablespoons butter, divided

1 lemon, cut into wedges, optional

DID YOU KNOW?

Skinless chicken breasts are an excellent source of lean protein. Cooking over medium heat for a short period of time gives them a tasty brown coating without overcooking the inside.

HELPING HANDS

Young children can help beat the egg, older ones can pound the chicken and soak it in the egg mixture. Make sure they wash their hands with soap and water after handling raw chicken!

Beat egg and milk in a small bowl with a fork. Add salt and pepper. Place chicken fillets in egg mixture and mix so all pieces become coated.

Place bread crumbs on a large plate. Dip each chicken piece into the breadcrumbs. Turn to coat both sides, patting gently to remove excess crumbs. Place on a separate plate. Repeat until all chicken is coated.

Melt 2 tablespoons butter in a nonstick skillet over medium heat.

When butter begins to foam, place half the chicken in the pan and cook for 3 to 4 minutes. Turn chicken and cook for 3 to 4 minutes more until it is thoroughly cooked. Remove to a serving plate. Repeat with remaining butter and chicken pieces. Garnish with lemon wedges.

VARIATIONS Substitute thinly sliced turkey breast for the chicken. Or add ¼ cup grated Parmesan cheese to the breadcrumbs and cook over low heat so the cheese does not burn.

Fresh Berry Tart

PREP TIME: 40 MINUTES **REST TIME:** 30 MINUTES **COOK TIME:** 30 MINUTES **SERVES** 16

This family-friendly dessert made with a shortbread crust, pastry cream and fresh berries looks fancy and elegant, yet it is straightforward to prepare. Make the pastry cream and crust ahead of time and assemble just before serving.

FOR THE CRUST:

3½ cups all-purpose flour

1½ cups sugar

Pinch of sea salt

Zest of 1 lemon

1 large egg

1 large egg yolk

1½ cups butter, 3 sticks, room temperature, cut into small chunks

FOR THE PASTRY CREAM:

4 egg yolks

4 tablespoons sugar

Zest of one lemon OR 1 teaspoon pure vanilla extract

4 tablespoons all-purpose flour OR 3 tablespoons cornstarch

2 cups milk

2 tablespoons butter

FOR THE GARNISH:

1 pint blueberries

1 pint raspberries

1 pint strawberries OR your favorite fruit

½ cup powdered sugar

DID YOU KNOW?

Colorful berries are rich in disease-fighting antioxidants and the tiny seeds are a good source of fiber.

KITCHEN TIP:

Be careful, pastry cream will curdle if it is cooked at too high a temperature.

PREPARE THE CRUST:

Place flour, sugar, salt and lemon zest in the bowl of an electric mixer fitted with a paddle attachment. Stir together with a spoon and make an indentation in the middle. Add one egg and one egg yolk. Add the room-temperature butter and beat gently for 30 seconds. Scrape the sides and bottom with a rubber spatula to make sure all the ingredients are well mixed.

Transfer half the dough to a large piece of plastic wrap. Flatten into a disc about 6 inches in diameter. Wrap tightly. Repeat. Refrigerate both discs for 30 minutes.

Preheat oven to 400°F.

Remove dough from refrigerator.

Place a large sheet of plastic wrap on the counter. Sprinkle lightly with flour. Place disc of dough on plastic, lightly sprinkle dough with flour, then pat with your fingers to make an 8-inch disc. Cover with a second piece of plastic wrap. With a rolling pin, roll the dough a few times in one direction, then turn entire assembly a quarter turn and roll some more. Continue until you have a 13-inch circle. Do not overwork the dough!

Remove the top piece of plastic, lift the bottom piece of plastic and flip the dough into a 10 or 12-inch tart pan. Lightly press the dough gently and evenly. Remove any overhanging dough by rolling the pin across the top. Patch any holes with extra dough. Crimp edges and prick dough with a fork. You can instead make six 4-inch individual tarts. Repeat with the remaining dough or freeze for up to three months.

Bake for 12 to 15 minutes, or until the edges are lightly browned. Allow to cool completely before filling.

PREPARE THE PASTRY CREAM:
Place the egg yolks and sugar in a heavy-bottomed, medium saucepan and beat with a whisk until all the sugar is dissolved, at least 5 minutes! Add lemon zest or vanilla extract.

Add flour (or cornstarch) a little at a time to the egg mixture and beat well. Add ¼ cup milk, mix well. Slowly add remaining milk, stirring continuously until well mixed.

Place pan on low to medium heat and bring to a low boil, stirring constantly. Let boil gently for 1 minute. Remove from heat and stir in butter. Let cool for a couple of minutes, then place a sheet of plastic wrap directly on the custard so it will not form a skin as it cools.

Spoon cooled pastry cream into cooled crust. Decorate with fresh berries. Dust with powdered sugar.

KITCHEN TIP:
To keep your crust flaky, do not overwork the dough.

HELPING HANDS
Children can spread dough in the tart pan, help rinse the berries and arrange the fruit.

Spinach Frittata

PREP TIME: 10 MINUTES **COOK TIME:** 20 MINUTES **SERVES:** 8

- 3 pounds fresh spinach, rinsed OR one 16-ounce package frozen chopped spinach
- 3 tablespoons olive oil, divided
- 4 large eggs
- ½ teaspoon sea salt
- Dash freshly ground pepper
- ¾ cup grated Parmesan cheese

If you are using fresh spinach, put it in a large pot with 2 cups of boiling water. Cover and cook over high heat for 4 to 5 minutes, stirring often. Remove from heat, drain and let cool. Squeeze out any excess water.

If you are using frozen spinach, defrost it and drain well. Squeeze out any excess water. In a bowl beat eggs, salt and pepper. Stir in the spinach, parmesan and bread crumbs.

Heat 2 tablespoons oil in a large nonstick skillet, over medium heat. Pour the egg mixture in the skillet. Cover and cook for 6 to 8 minutes on low heat. Using a lid or a large flat plate, slide the frittata out of the pan onto the plate or lid, then add remaining tablespoon olive oil and carefully flip the frittata over back into the same skillet. Cover and cook for 5 more minutes.

Remove to a serving plate, let cool and cut into wedges.

DID YOU KNOW?

Rich, leafy, dark-green spinach is considered to be a cancer fighter, a mental stimulant and an immune booster.

HELPING HANDS

Young children can help crack the eggs. Older ones can beat them.

KITCHEN TIP:

Flipping the frittata can be a little tricky. So you can bake it instead. Pour the mixture into a greased baking pan and bake for 45 minutes at 325°F.

{ **VARIATIONS** Substitute Swiss chard for the spinach. }

Tri-tip Panino

PREP TIME: 10 MINUTES **COOK TIME:** 20 MINUTES **SERVES:** 4

Another winner! All of your friends will ask you for the recipe of this panino. It's true! Need is the mother of all inventions. We created this delicious combination to conquer the hungry stomachs of many of our male customers. We discovered that men love meat, cheese and onions.

4 dutch crunch or sourdough rolls

1 pound tri-tip, cut across the grain into approx. $\frac{1}{4}$-inch thick slices

2 zucchini squash, rinsed and cut lengthwise into $\frac{1}{8}$-inch slices

2 tablespoons olive oil

1 large red onion, peeled and cut into $\frac{1}{4}$-inch slices

1 tablespoon balsamic vinegar

4 slices provolone or pepperjack cheese

Sea salt and freshly ground pepper to taste

DID YOU KNOW?
You can use left over steak to make this sandwich.

HELPING HANDS
Children can help layer the panino filling.

CURIOSITY:
In Italian, "panino" means sandwich and "panini" means sandwiches.

Prepare a hot grill. Generously sprinkle the slices of tri-tip with salt and pepper on both sides and grill for 3 to 4 minutes per side. Remove to a plate.

Repeat with the zucchini and grill 3 to 4 minutes per side. Remove to a plate.

Meanwhile, heat olive oil in a large nonstick skillet, over low to medium heat. Add the onions and cook for 10 minutes. Add balsamic vinegar, reduce heat to low and continue cooking for 10 more minutes, stirring occasionally. Add salt and pepper. Turn off the heat and add grilled zucchini to the pan. Stir to coat.

Fill each roll with 2 to 3 slices of tri-tip (for better results warm up the bread in the oven) a few slices of zucchini, some onions and a slice of cheese. Serve immediately.

soups
AND
salads

WE KNOW the kitchen is not only where we cook but also where family and friends hang out, tell stories and bond through the sharing of food. It is a friendly place that provides opportunities to strengthen relationships through everyday interaction.

Tomato, Cucumber & Red Onion Salad

PREP TIME: 10 MINUTES **SERVES:** 4

There's nothing more refreshing than a light, delicious salad. The cool crunch of the cucumber paired with the sweet tomato flavor and tangy bite of the red onion is a classic combination.

FOR THE SALAD:

2 large ripe tomatoes, rinsed and cut into small wedges

1 large cucumber, rinsed and cut into $1/4$-inch half-moons

$1/2$ small red onion, peeled and cut into $1/8$-inch slices

2 tablespoons fresh mint, chopped fine

FOR THE DRESSING:

1 tablespoon balsamic vinegar

$1/4$ teaspoon sea salt

Dash freshly ground pepper

$1/3$ cup extra-virgin olive oil

FOR THE GARNISH:

$1/2$ cup crumbled feta cheese, optional

PREPARE THE DRESSING:

Pour vinegar into a small bowl. Stir in salt and pepper. Whisking continuously, slowly add the olive oil until it is thoroughly blended. Taste and adjust for salt and pepper.

PREPARE THE SALAD:

Place tomatoes, cucumber, onion and mint in a serving bowl.

Toss with vegetables. Garnishing with feta is optional.

CURIOSITY:

Cucumbers wrapped in plastic are an English variety that are not waxed, have less seeds and are more easily digested.

HELPING HANDS

Children can help toss the salad.

KITCHEN TIP:

Adjust the seasonings to compliment the flavor of the tomato. The sweetness changes depending on the variety and the season.

Pasta e Fagioli Soup

PREP TIME: 15 MINUTES **COOK TIME:** 60 MINUTES **SERVES:** 6

Pasta e Fagioli is a great winter soup. The original recipe uses borlotti (cranberry) beans, but you can substitute cannellini beans for a more subtle taste.

DID YOU KNOW?

Beans or legumes are rich in soluble fiber, minerals, protein and vitamin A.

HELPING HANDS

Young children can help rinse the carrot and celery.

CURIOSITY:

History reveals that this soup was created by the Venetians, as they were the first to import these beans from the Americas.

1 15-ounce can cannellini beans, drained

¼ cup olive oil

1 onion, peeled and chopped fine, about 1 cup

2 garlic cloves, peeled and minced

1 large carrot, peeled and chopped fine

1 celery rib, rinsed and chopped fine

4 cups chicken or vegetable broth, warmed

½ teaspoon dried thyme

½ teaspoon dried oregano

½ teaspoon dried marjoram

4 fresh sage leaves

½ teaspoon sea salt

3 ounces small dried pasta

2 tablespoons fresh parsley, chopped fine

Dash freshly ground pepper

FOR THE GARNISH:

Freshly grated Parmesan cheese

Extra-virgin olive oil

Set aside one cup of beans and mash the rest.

Heat olive oil in a large pot over medium heat. Add onion, garlic, carrots and celery, and sauté for 5 minutes. Add ½ cup of broth and sauté for 5 more minutes. Add another ½ cup of broth, whole canned beans, dried herbs and fresh sage. Cook for a few minutes so the beans soak up the flavors.

Add the remaining broth and the mashed beans. Bring to a gentle boil, let cook for 30 to 40 minutes. Add salt and pasta. Cook stirring occasionally until the pasta is done. (You may need to add more broth as the pasta will absorb some liquid as it cooks.)

Add the parsley and pepper. Taste and adjust for salt and pepper. Serve with Parmesan cheese and a drizzle of extra-virgin olive oil.

Butternut Squash Soup

PREP TIME: 45 MINUTES   **COOK TIME:** 30 MINUTES   **SERVES:** 4

Endless flavor combinations exist for creating a delicious soup with this very humble vegetable. Roasting the squash, prior to boiling it, intensifies the wonderful flavor.

1 medium butternut squash, about 2 pounds

2 tablespoons olive oil

½ onion, peeled and chopped fine, about ½ cup

½ teaspoon sea salt

¼ teaspoon freshly ground pepper

½ teaspoon ground ginger OR ¼ teaspoon curry powder

3 cups chicken broth

½ cup half and half, optional

Homemade focaccia croutons, optional pg 232

DID YOU KNOW?

Butternut squash is a great source of vitamin A, vitamin C, potassium and manganese.

HELPING HANDS

Young children can help sprinkle the croutons. Older ones can remove the pulp from the skin when cooked.

KITCHEN TIP:

To soften the skin, place the whole squash in the microwave and cook for 1 to 2 minutes prior to cutting.

PREPARE THE SQUASH:

Preheat oven to 400°F.

Rinse squash and cut in 1-inch discs. Lay squash in a baking pan. Brush cut surfaces with a little olive oil. Bake for 30 to 45 minutes or until soft. When cool to the touch, using a large spoon, scoop out and discard seeds. Remove pulp from skin. You should have about 2 cups of pulp.

Heat olive oil in a large saucepan over low to medium heat. Add onion and sauté until translucent, about 5 minutes. Add squash and continue cooking for 10 minutes, stirring occasionally. Season with salt, pepper, ginger or curry.

Add chicken broth and bring the soup to a gentle boil. Cook for 2 minutes.

Remove from heat and blend soup with an immersion blender or in small batches in a standard blender. Be careful when blending hot liquids! *Blend in small batches! The heat in the soup will cause the mixture to expand. The soup could explode out of the blender and burn you.*

Return soup to saucepan, add half and half, optional. Reheat over low heat until the soup barely boils. Taste and adjust for salt and pepper.

Ladle into bowls and sprinkle with homemade focaccia croutons.

Caprese Salad

PREP TIME: 10 MINUTES **SERVES:** 4

This dish has the colors of the Italian flag – red, white and green. It takes its name from where it originates, the island of Capri, located off the southern coast of Italy.

2 medium tomatoes, the best you can find!

1 8-ounce ball fresh mozzarella

6 fresh basil leaves

¼ cup extra-virgin olive oil

Sea salt

Freshly ground pepper

Slice the tomatoes in ½-inch rounds. Slice the mozzarella in ½-inch rounds.

Arrange on a serving plate, alternating the tomato slices with the mozzarella. Tear the basil with your fingers and sprinkle it on top. Drizzle with olive oil and season with salt and pepper. Serve immediately.

DID YOU KNOW?

The word "mozzarella" comes from the italian verb "mozzare" – the name of the movement it takes to make this cheese out of raw milk.

HELPING HANDS

Young children can help rinse the tomatoes and tear the basil. Older ones can cut the mozzarella and the tomatoes with supervision.

KITCHEN TIP:

Ideally, the mozzarella in this recipe should be Mozzarella di Bufala, fresh cheese made from water buffalo milk. If you can't find it, use fresh mozzarella.

Chopped Chicken Salad

PREP TIME: 15 MINUTES **SERVES:** 4 TO 6

This salad was created because Eddie, Rima's cousin, insisted that we serve a chopped salad at the restaurant. We made up the salad and our resourceful manager, Saul, gave us his family's dressing recipe. Eddie was right, it became an instant success!

FOR THE SALAD:

½ head iceberg lettuce, rinsed, drained and chopped fine

¼ head red cabbage, rinsed, drained and chopped fine

½ cucumber, rinsed, peeled and sliced thin

¼ small red onion, finely chopped

1 cup canned garbanzo beans, drained

½ cup cooked or canned corn

2 cups grilled or cooked chicken, cut into small cubes, about
  4 boneless, skinless chicken breast halves

½ cup feta cheese

FOR THE DRESSING:

½ cup extra-virgin olive oil

½ cup frozen cranberry juice cocktail, concentrate

½ teaspoon sea salt

1 tablespoon white wine vinegar

Juice of ½ lemon

DID YOU KNOW?

Cranberries contain condensed tannins. This humble fruit can protect against ulcers and gum disease.

HELPING HANDS

Young children can help toss the salad. Older ones can rinse the vegetables and make the dressing.

KITCHEN TIP:

After blending the dressing ingredients, toss and serve the salad immediately!

PREPARE THE DRESSING:
Combine dressing ingredients in a blender. Taste and adjust for salt.

PREPARE THE SALAD:
Place salad ingredients in a large bowl, including chicken. Toss with the dressing. Sprinkle with feta cheese. Serve immediately.

Bella Salad

PREP TIME: 10 MINUTES **SERVES:** 4

The flavor of this sweet basil dressing is fresh and tangy. Its pleasing aroma and bright color creates a completely new chicken salad experience. This recipe highlights the versatility of this popular herb.

FOR THE SALAD:

6 cups mixed greens, about 5 ounces, rinsed and dried

2 cups grilled or cooked chicken, cut into small cubes, about 4 boneless, skinless chicken breast halves

8 asparagus spears, steamed and cut into thirds

½ cup cooked or canned corn

½ cup pine nuts

½ cup shaved Parmesan cheese

2 cups potato chips

FOR THE DRESSING:

2 cups fresh basil leaves, packed, about 1½ ounces, washed and air-dried or spun in the salad spinner

⅔ cup extra-virgin olive oil

½ teaspoon sea salt

1 garlic clove, peeled

PREPARE THE DRESSING:

Combine basil leaves, olive oil, salt and garlic in a food processor fitted with a steel blade. Process for 30 seconds.

PREPARE THE SALAD:

Place salad ingredients in a large bowl. Toss with half of the dressing, add more to taste. Sprinkle with shaved Parmesan and potato chips. Serve immediately.

DID YOU KNOW?

Basil has many medicinal purposes. Its strong taste and smell actually aides the digestive process.

HELPING HANDS

Young children can help pick the basil leaves, rinse them and dry them. Older ones can make the dressing.

CURIOSITY:

Often associated with Italian cooking, basil is native to the far eastern countries of India, Pakistan and Thailand.

Mixed Greens

PREP TIME: 10 MINUTES **SERVES:** 4

Assorted mixed greens are readily available at most supermarkets.

FOR THE SALAD:

6 cups mixed greens, about 5 ounces, rinsed and dried

FOR THE DRESSING:

⅓ cup balsamic vinegar

¼ teaspoon sea salt

Dash freshly ground pepper

1 cup extra-virgin olive oil

PREPARE THE DRESSING:

Pour vinegar into a small bowl. Stir in salt and pepper. Whisking continuously, slowly add the olive oil until it is thoroughly blended.

PREPARE THE SALAD:

Place salad greens in a large bowl. Toss with one third of the dressing. Taste and adjust for salt, pepper and/or dressing. Serve immediately. (Store extra dressing in the refrigerator, shake well before using.)

DID YOU KNOW?

In Europe a green salad is served after the main course.

HELPING HANDS

Young children can help spin the salad greens. Older ones can make the dressing.

Scampi e Fagioli

PREP TIME: 5 MINUTES **COOK TIME:** 20 MINUTES **REST TIME:** 20 MINUTES **SERVES:** 4

At Café Luna we offered a variety of dishes from the Italian Riviera tradition. This recipe from the Versilia area, where Rima is from, was a big success! Our friend, Giuliano, serves the best version at his restaurant, Da Madeo in Forte dei Marmi, Italy.

FOR THE SALAD:

1 15-ounce can cannellini beans, drained

2 tablespoons extra-virgin olive oil

1 garlic clove, peeled and minced

2 fresh sage leaves

¼ teaspoon sea salt

1 pound fresh, medium uncooked prawns, shelled and deveined, OR 1 pound frozen, medium uncooked prawns, tail-off

¼ teaspoon sea salt

1 small tomato, rinsed and chopped into small pieces

1 cup arugula leaves, about 1 ounce, rinsed and dried

FOR THE DRESSING:

½ cup extra-virgin olive oil

2 tablespoons fresh lemon juice (1 lemon)

¼ teaspoon sea salt

Dash freshly ground pepper

Heat olive oil in a medium saucepan over low to medium heat. Add minced garlic and sage and sauté for 1 minute. Add cannellini beans, ¼ cup water and salt. Reduce heat to low, cover and simmer for 10 minutes.

Meanwhile, prepare the prawns: place 2 quarts of water in a large saucepan and bring to a boil. Add fresh or frozen prawns and salt. Turn off the heat, cover and let sit for 5 to 7 minutes. Drain.

In a small bowl, whisk the olive oil with the lemon juice, salt and pepper until thoroughly mixed. Mix the cooked and drained prawns with one half of the dressing. Let marinate at room temperature for 20 minutes.

TO SERVE:

Place the beans in a deep serving platter. Cover with remaining dressing. Top with marinated prawns and garnish with chopped tomatoes and arugula leaves. Serve immediately.

Minestrone

PREP TIME: 20 MINUTES **COOK TIME:** 70 MINUTES **SERVES:** 8

This recipe was given to us by a very good friend. We did change it a little but the result is still unbelievable!

¼ cup olive oil

½ onion, chopped fine, about ½ cup

I carrot, peeled and diced

I celery rib, rinsed and diced

I tablespoon fresh parsley, chopped fine

I small sprig fresh oregano OR I teaspoon dried

I small sprig fresh rosemary OR I teaspoon dried

I small sprig fresh thyme OR I teaspoon dried

2 teaspoons sea salt

I 15-ounce can, good quality, plain tomato sauce

I medium zucchini, rinsed and diced

I medium potato, peeled and diced

I leek, rinsed and chopped into thin slices

¼ pound fresh green beans, rinsed and cut into I-inch pieces

¼ cabbage, rinsed and chopped into thin slices

I cup canned small white beans OR cannellini beans

I cup small pasta, such as anellini or macaroni

½ cup freshly grated Parmesan cheese

DID YOU KNOW?

Cooking the vegetables in stages, with the herbs and tomato sauce, allows the flavors to develop more fully. Like most hearty soups, minestrone is better the second day.

HELPING HANDS

Young children can help rinse the vegetables. Older ones can cut them with supervision.

CURIOSITY:

Thyme contains thymol, an oil with therapeutic effects against coughs and bronchitis.

Heat olive oil in a large 6-quart stock pot over medium heat. Add onion, carrot and celery, and sauté for 5 to 8 minutes.

Add herbs and salt. Sauté for more 2 minutes. Add tomato sauce and continue cooking. After 5 minutes, add zucchini, potato, leek, green beans and cabbage. Cook for 5 more minutes, stirring often.

Add 6 cups of water. Bring to a boil. Reduce heat to low, cover and simmer for 40 minutes, stirring occasionally.

Add beans and pasta and cook for 10 more minutes. Taste and adjust for salt. Sprinkle with freshly grated Parmesan cheese.

Buonissima Salad

PREP TIME: 20 MINUTES **SERVES:** 4 TO 6

We could never make enough of this great tasting, healthy and filling salad at our restaurant, Café Luna. It was a best-seller!

FOR THE SALAD:

2 cups grilled or cooked chicken, cut into small cubes, about 4 boneless, skinless chicken breast halves

I head romaine lettuce, rinsed, dried, cut in I-inch pieces

I avocado, peeled and chopped into small pieces

I tomato, rinsed and chopped into small pieces

2 large eggs, boiled, peeled and chopped

I cup blue cheese crumbles

FOR THE DRESSING:

2 tablespoons balsamic vinegar

I tablespoon Dijon mustard

$^{1}/_{4}$ teaspoon sea salt

Dash freshly ground pepper

$^{1}/_{2}$ cup extra-virgin olive oil

PREPARE THE DRESSING:

Combine vinegar, mustard, salt and pepper in a small bowl. Whisking continuously, slowly add the olive oil until it is thoroughly blended with the vinegar. (You can also use a hand-held mixer or blender.) Taste and adjust for salt and pepper.

PREPARE THE SALAD:

Place lettuce in a large salad bowl and toss it with half the dressing. Add the chicken, then layer the remaining salad ingredients: tomato, avocado, chopped egg and blue cheese. Drizzle the remaining dressing on top of the salad.

Caesar Salad

PREP TIME: 15 MINUTES **SERVES:** 4 TO 6

Caesar dressing has no relation to Julius or any of his Roman compatriots. It was created in the early 1900s by Caesar Cardini, a restaurateur in Tijuana, Mexico. The real debate is not over its origin, but whether the original recipe had anchovies or not.

DID YOU KNOW?

Adding the oil to the egg mixture in a slow, steady stream helps to emulsify the dressing.

KITCHEN TIP:

Young children and people in at-risk health groups should avoid eating foods that contain raw or lightly-cooked eggs.

FOR THE SALAD:

2 heads romaine lettuce, rinsed and dried

1 cup shaved Parmesan cheese

1 cup croutons, pg 232

FOR THE DRESSING:

2 large egg yolks

1 tablespoon Dijon mustard

Juice of one lemon

1 garlic clove, peeled and crushed

⅓ anchovy

½ teaspoon sea salt

1 teaspoon freshly ground pepper

1 cup olive oil, not extra-virgin

½ cup freshly grated Parmesan cheese

PREPARE THE DRESSING:

Combine egg yolks, mustard, lemon juice, garlic, anchovy, salt and pepper in a blender.

With the blender running on low speed, add olive oil in a slow stream until it is well emulsified. Taste and adjust for salt and pepper. Add ½ cup freshly grated Parmesan cheese. Keep refrigerated until ready to use.

PREPARE THE SALAD:

Tear lettuce into bite-size pieces and place in a large bowl. Toss with dressing. Sprinkle with shaved Parmesan cheese and croutons.

Garden Salad

PREP TIME: 10 MINUTES **SERVES:** 6

A garden salad tastes great any time of the year. This version features produce that can be grown in a home garden.

FOR THE SALAD:

1 head green leaf lettuce, rinsed and dried

1 tomato, rinsed and chopped

1 carrot, peeled and grated

4 radishes, rinsed and sliced thin

1 cup canned kidney beans, drained

1 tablespoon chopped red onion, optional

½ cup blue cheese crumbles, optional

½ bell pepper, rinsed and thinly sliced, optional

FOR THE DRESSING:

⅓ cup balsamic vinegar

¼ teaspoon sea salt

Dash freshly ground pepper

1 cup extra-virgin olive oil

DID YOU KNOW?

Radishes are fat-and cholesterol-free and high in vitamins that contain sulfurous compounds that protect against cancer.

HELPING HANDS

Young children can help grow and pick the vegetables. Older ones can make the dressing.

KITCHEN TIP:

To remove excess water, place chopped tomatoes in a small bowl and sprinkle with salt. Drain after 10 minutes.

PREPARE THE DRESSING:

Pour vinegar into a small bowl. Stir in salt and pepper. Whisking continuously, slowly add the olive oil until it is thoroughly blended.

PREPARE THE SALAD:

Tear lettuce leaves and place in a large bowl. Add tomato, carrot, radishes, kidney beans and optional ingredients. Toss with one third of the dressing. Taste and adjust for salt, pepper and/or dressing. Serve immediately. Store extra dressing in the refrigerator, shake well before using.

Avocado, Carrot, Potato & Green Beans

PREP TIME: 5 MINUTES   **COOK TIME:** 15 MINUTES   **REST TIME:** 60 MINUTES   **SERVES:** 4 TO 6

Ever since Rima's mom, Malak, created this recipe for a family dinner, it has become a staple in our summer meals.

FOR THE SALAD:

1 large russet potato, peeled and cut into 2-inch cubes

2 large carrots, peeled and cut into 1-inch rounds

¼ pound fresh green beans, rinsed, tips removed and cut in half

2 avocados, peeled and chopped into 1-inch pieces

FOR THE DRESSING:

½ cup pesto, pg 120

½ cup extra-virgin olive oil

½ teaspoon sea salt

Place 2 cups of water in a large saucepan. Add potato and bring to a boil. Cook for 10 to 15 minutes until it breaks easily when pierced with a fork. Remove from heat and drain in a colander.

Place 2 cups of water in a saucepan. Add chopped carrots and bring to a boil. Cook for 8 to 10 minutes until soft. Remove from heat and drain in a colander.

Place 2 cups of water in a saucepan. Bring to a boil. Add green beans and cook for 3 minutes. Remove from heat and drain in a colander.

Transfer vegetables to a serving bowl. Let cool to room temperature, about 1 hour.

In a small bowl, combine pesto, olive oil and salt. Add avocado to the vegetables. Pour dressing over vegetables and toss. Taste and adjust for salt. Serve at room temperature or chill and serve cold.

DID YOU KNOW?

Green beans are a good source of A and B-complex vitamins, calcium and potassium. A fresh bean should snap crisply and be velvety to the touch.

HELPING HANDS

Children can grow an avocado tree by placing a clean pit in a glass filled with water. (Push 3 toothpicks evenly around the middle to make a base so it doesn't sink to the bottom.)

KITCHEN TIP:

If preparing ahead, do not peel and chop the avocado until you are ready to serve the salad.

Creamy Tomato Soup

PREP TIME: 10 MINUTES **COOK TIME:** 40 MINUTES **SERVES:** 4 TO 6

The combination of sautéed vegetables, white wine and tomatoes gives this soup a satisfying flavor. It is sure to become your family's favorite tomato soup.

DID YOU KNOW?

When choosing your tomatoes, be sure to pick those with the most brilliant shades of red. These indicate the highest amounts of betacarotene and lycopene.

HELPING HANDS

Young children can help rinse the carrot and celery and measure the herbs.

KITCHEN TIP:

Substitute 1 teaspoon dried Italian seasoning for the fresh herbs.

¼ cup olive oil

1 garlic clove, peeled and minced

½ onion, peeled and chopped fine, about ½ cup

1 carrot, peeled and chopped fine

1 celery rib, rinsed and chopped fine

4 fresh basil leaves

1 small sprig fresh oregano

1 small sprig fresh thyme

½ teaspoon sea salt

Dash freshly ground pepper

½ cup dry white wine

1 28-oz can, good quality diced tomatoes

2 cups chicken broth

½ cup heavy whipping cream, optional

Heat olive oil in a large saucepan over medium heat. Add garlic, onion, carrot and celery. Sauté for 5 to 8 minutes, stirring often. Add herbs, salt, pepper and white wine, reduce heat to low and cook for 5 more minutes.

Add diced tomatoes and 1 cup chicken broth. Bring to a boil, stirring occasionally. Reduce heat, cover, and simmer for 20 minutes. Remove frm heat.

Remove herbs and blend soup with an immersion blender or in small batches in a standard blender. Be careful when blending hot liquids! *Blend in small batches! The heat in the soup will cause the mixture to expand. The soup could explode out of the blender and burn you.*

Add remaining broth and cream, optional. Reheat over low heat until the soup barely boils. Taste and adjust for salt and pepper.

Tri-tip Salad

PREP TIME: 10 MINUTES **COOK TIME:** 8 TO 10 MINUTES **SERVES:** 4

Slices of grilled tri-tip served on a bed of fresh greens is every man's favorite salad. At Café Luna, when men were hungry but watching their diet, they would always order this delicious meal.

1 pound tri-tip, cut in ¼-inch slices
  (Cut meat across the grain, starting at the short end.)

Sea salt and freshly ground pepper

1 head romaine lettuce, rinsed well and chopped into bite-size pieces

2 large tomatoes, rinsed and cut into small pieces

1 cup blue cheese crumbles

2 cups potato chips

2 tablespoons parsley, optional

FOR THE DRESSING:

2 tablespoons balsamic vinegar

1 tablespoon Dijon mustard

¼ teaspoon sea salt

Dash freshly ground pepper

½ cup extra-virgin olive oil

DID YOU KNOW?

The tri-tip roast or steak, also called a triangle roast, has great flavor and tends to be lower in fat than most other cuts.

HELPING HANDS

Young children can wash and cut the lettuce. Older ones can make the dressing.

PREPARE THE STEAK:

Prepare a hot grill. Sprinkle the slices of tri-tip generously with salt and pepper on both sides. Place meat on the grill and cook 2 to 3 minutes per side.

PREPARE THE DRESSING:

Combine vinegar, mustard, salt and pepper in a small bowl. Whisking continuously, slowly add the olive oil until it is thoroughly blended with the vinegar. (You can also use a hand-held mixer or blender.) Taste and adjust for salt and pepper.

PREPARE THE SALAD:

Place the lettuce in a large bowl and toss with half the dressing. Add tomatoes, blue cheese and grilled tri-tip. Drizzle with remaining dressing. Garnish with potato chips and parsley. Serve immediately.

VARIATIONS Thin slices of leftover fillet or New York steak work great with this salad.

pasta AND grains

WE KNOW that time spent with our kids is irreplaceable. The kitchen is a wonderful place to teach life-long skills, pass on traditional recipes, bake a memory and decorate a dream.

Penne Arrabbiata

PREP TIME: 5 MINUTES **COOK TIME:** 20 MINUTES **SERVES:** 4 TO 6

The simplicity of this Roman recipe reflects the genuine Mediterranean lifestyle.

DID YOU KNOW?

In Italian, "arrabbiata" means angry. This dish is not really "angry," just a touch spicy.

HELPING HANDS

Young children can help set the table. They should not be allowed too close to the stove.

1 pound penne pasta

4 tablespoons extra-virgin olive oil

2 garlic cloves, peeled

1 teaspoon crushed red hot chili peppers flakes OR 2 peppercorns

1 15-ounce can, good quality, diced tomatoes

¼ teaspoon sea salt

½ cup freshly grated Parmesan cheese

Heat olive oil in a large sauté pan over low to medium heat. Add garlic and pepper flakes, reduce heat and sauté for 2 minutes. The key for the success of this dish is to cook the garlic and the pepper without burning them!

Add diced tomatoes and salt. Cover, bring to boil, reduce heat to low and cook for 15 minutes, stirring occasionally.

Meanwhile, start cooking the penne. Bring 4 quarts of water to a boil in a large pot over high heat. When the water is boiling, add 2 tablespoons salt and penne. Reduce heat to medium-high and cook uncovered, stirring occasionally.

When penne are 3 minutes from being done, transfer them to the sauce in the skillet using a slotted spoon. Add about ½ cup of the cooking water and cook for a few minutes over medium heat, stirring often and adding more water if necessary. The pasta will finish cooking in the sauce. Taste and adjust for salt and pepper flakes. Sprinkle with Parmesan cheese and serve.

Lasagna

PREP TIME: 20 MINUTES **COOK TIME:** 60 MINUTES **REST TIME:** 20 MINUTES **SERVES:** 8

Lasagna is a great family dish. This world-famous recipe is from Malak, Rima's mom. Traditional Italian lasagna is made with tomato meat ragu and Béchamel white sauce.

½ pound, about 9, lasagna pasta sheets

4½ cups, 1 batch, Béchamel White Sauce, pg 97

4 cups, ½ batch, Tomato Meat Ragu, pg 98

1 cup shredded mozzarella cheese, optional

½ cup freshly grated Parmesan cheese

KITCHEN TIP:

If you use "no-boiling required" lasagna pasta, leave the Ragu Tomato Meat Sauce a little more liquid. It will help the lasagna stay moist.

HELPING HANDS

Children can help swirl the sauces together and sprinkle the Parmesan cheese.

Preheat oven to 350°F.

In a large pot, bring 4 quarts water to boil over high heat. Add 2 tablespoons salt. Add lasagna sheets and cook for 10 minutes, stirring occasionally. Remove from heat and drain. Place cooked pasta sheets in a bowl of ice water for a few minutes or until cool enough to handle. Drain, then use immediately.

ASSEMBLE THE LASAGNA:

Place three cooked and drained sheets in the bottom of a 9 x 13-inch baking pan, overlapping if necessary. (No-boiling required pasta does not need to be cooked.) Cover with 1½ cups Tomato Meat Ragu and 1¼ cups Béchamel White Sauce. Swirl sauces together with a large spoon.

Sprinkle evenly with ½ cup mozzarella, optional.

Make a second layer in the same manner.

Top with remaining three cooked noodles. Cover with 1 cup Tomato Meat Ragu and 1 cup Béchamel White Sauce, swirl together. Top with remaining Béchamel White Sauce. Sprinkle with Parmesan cheese.

Bake in preheated oven for 40 to 45 minutes if using fresh pasta or 50 to 55 minutes if using no-boiling required pasta. Broil for 5 more minutes or until top is golden brown. Let rest 20 minutes before serving.

Cover pasta with Tomato Meat Ragu

Add Bechamel White Sauce

Swirl sauces together

Sprinkle with shredded mozzarella

Tomato Meat Ragu

PREP TIME: 10 MINUTES   **COOK TIME:** 2 HOURS 30 MINUTES   **MAKES:** 8 CUPS

Every Italian family has a favorite version of this classic sauce made with ground meat, onions, celery, carrots, tomatoes and red wine. Rima's family recipe is much simpler. When her father, Badi, and his friend, Riccardo, were working in Kuwait in the 1950's there were few vegetables, and definitely no wine. All they had were onions, tomato sauce, ground beef and lots of time to let their sauce simmer. That is how this great yet simple recipe was created!

CUROSITY:

In Naples, the sauce is nicknamed "guadaporta," for the doorman who has time to watch the sauce while watching the door.

DID YOU KNOW?

The word "ragu" is a blend of the French word for stew, or "ragout," and the Latin word for taste, "gustus."

¼ cup extra-virgin olive oil

1 onion, peeled and finely chopped, about 1 cup

1 pound lean ground beef

¼ teaspoon sea salt

⅛ teaspoon freshly ground pepper

2 15-ounce cans, good quality tomato sauce

1 can water (use empty tomato sauce can)

3 tablespoons tomato paste

Heat the olive oil in a large saucepan over medium heat. Add the onion and sauté for 5 minutes over medium-low heat until translucent.

Add the ground beef and cook over medium-low heat, breaking it up with a wooden spoon, for 10 to 12 minutes. Stir in salt and pepper.

Add the tomato sauce, water and tomato paste. Stir well. Bring to a boil. Reduce heat, cover and simmer on low heat for 2 hours, stirring every 30 minutes. Remove cover and simmer for 15 more minutes or until some oil rises to the top of the sauce. Taste and adjust for salt and pepper.

Remove from heat. Serve over cooked and drained pasta or use to make lasagna. Allow to cool and refrigerate for up to five days, or freeze in resealable plastic bags for up to three months.

Béchamel White Sauce

COOK TIME: 20 MINUTES   **MAKES:** 4½ CUPS

This classic white sauce is made from butter, flour and milk. It is used as a base for many dishes such as lasagna, pasticcio and homemade "mac & cheese."

- 4 cups milk
- ½ cup butter
- ½ cup flour
- 1 teaspoon salt
- ⅛ teaspoon ground nutmeg, better if freshly grated

Heat milk in a medium saucepan over low to medium heat to just below boiling point.

Meanwhile, melt the butter over low heat in a large saucepan. *(Be careful not to let it burn!)* When melted, remove from heat and whisk in the flour until well combined. Slowly whisk in heated milk.

Return to low heat. Add salt and nutmeg, and continue stirring until the sauce reaches a boil. Cook for three minutes, stirring constantly. Remove from heat.

NOTE:
Béchamel thickens as it cools. For a thinner consistency, use more milk.

CURIOSITY:

(bay-shah-mel) This sauce was created in the 14th century and was introduced by the Italian chefs of Catherine de Medici (1519-1589), the Italian-born Queen of France.

HELPING HANDS

Young children can measure the ingredients and older ones can stir the Béchamel.

{ **VARIATIONS** Substitute ¼ cup cornstarch for the flour and/or 4 cups chicken broth for the milk. }

Spaghetti al Ragu

COOK TIME: 10 MINUTES   **SERVES:** 4 TO 5

Twirling spaghetti on a fork can be tricky at first. Start with just a few strands and spin the fork until most of the spaghetti has formed a compact spiral. Enjoy the delicious mouthful and repeat.

1 pound spaghetti

2 tablespoons extra-virgin olive oil

3 to 4 cups Tomato Meat Ragu, pg 96

½ cup freshly grated Parmesan cheese

Bring 4 quarts of water to a boil in a large pot over high heat. When the water is boiling, add 2 tablespoons salt and spaghetti. Reduce heat to medium-high and cook uncovered, according to package directions, stirring occasionally.

Meanwhile, in a medium saucepan, warm the Tomato Meat Ragu over low heat, stirring occasionally. When spaghetti is cooked, drain and return it to the cooking pot. Toss with warm Tomato Meat Ragu and olive oil. Sprinkle with Parmesan cheese. Serve warm.

DID YOU KNOW?

Long-simmered tomato sauces are so delicious because the water has evaporated, leaving the flavors to blend together.

HELPING HANDS

Young children can help sprinkle the Parmesan cheese, older ones can grate it.

Orecchiette with Broccoli & Sun-dried Tomato

PREP TIME: 10 MINUTES **COOK TIME:** 20 MINUTES **SERVES:** 6 TO 8

Orecchiette is a type of pasta native to the Apulia region of Italy. Its shape resembles a small ear. Once made exclusively by hand, they can now be found in the pasta aisle of most grocery stores.

1 pound orecchiette pasta

¼ cup olive oil

1 garlic clove, peeled and minced

¼ pound broccoli florets, rinsed and steamed 5 minutes

¼ cup sun-dried tomatoes, oil-packed, julienne sliced

2 tablespoons fresh basil leaves, julienned

½ cup freshly grated Parmesan cheese

DID YOU KNOW?

Steamed broccoli has more vitamin C than an orange and as much calcium as a glass of milk. One medium cluster has three times more fiber than a slice of wheat bread.

HELPING HANDS

Young children can pick, wash and dry the basil, older ones can cut the broccoli with supervision.

CUROSITY

In Italian, "orecchio" means ear and "orecchiette" means little ears.

Heat olive oil in a small skillet over low to medium heat. Add garlic, broccoli, sun-dried tomatoes and basil. Cook for 5 minutes, stirring to coat broccoli.

Meanwhile, bring 4 quarts of water to a boil in a large pot over high heat. When the water is boiling, add 2 tablespoons salt and orecchiette. Reduce heat to medium-high and cook uncovered, according to package directions, stirring occasionally.

Drain pasta and toss with broccoli sauce. Sprinkle with Parmesan cheese and serve.

{ **VARIATIONS** Before serving, sprinkle with 2 tablespoons pine nuts that have been toasted in a hot oven for a few minutes. }

Barley with Shrimp & Scallops

PREP TIME: 5 MINUTES **COOK TIME:** 60 MINUTES **SERVES:** 6 TO 8

Barley is not just for soup! Cooking barley in plenty of water and then draining it like pasta produces a fluffy grain that can be served as a side with meat, or mixed with vegetables and fish in a salad.

I cup pearl barley

I teaspoon sea salt

4 tomatoes, rinsed and chopped into ½-inch dice

2 tablespoons extra-virgin olive oil

12 fresh basil leaves, chopped OR 2 tablespoons pesto, pg 120

I tablespoon olive oil

2 garlic cloves, peeled

½ pound bay scallops, rinsed and dried

I tablespoon flat-leaf parsley, minced

¼ to I teaspoon red pepper flakes

½ pound cooked bay shrimp, rinsed and dried

Additional fresh basil leaves, about 8

2 tablespoons pine nuts, toasted, optional

DID YOU KNOW?

Barley is a centuries-old grain with a rich nutlike flavor. This nutritious food is high in fiber and low in fat.

HELPING HANDS

Young children can help rinse the tomatoes and pick the basil. Older ones can rinse and dry the seafood.

Place 5 cups water, barley and salt in a large pot. Bring to a boil over high heat. Stir. Reduce heat, cover and simmer for 55 minutes. Drain in a colander. Set aside.

Meanwhile, place tomatoes in a large serving bowl. Mix with 2 tablespoons extra-virgin olive oil and chopped basil (or pesto.) Set aside.

Heat 1 tablespoon olive oil in a medium skillet. Add garlic cloves and pepper flakes and sauté over medium heat for 1 minute. Add scallops and parsley. Cook for 3 to 5 minutes, stirring so the scallops brown on all sides. Remove from heat. Discard garlic cloves.

Add shrimp, scallops and cooked barley to tomato mixture. Toss well.

Taste and adjust for olive oil, salt and pepper. Toss with remaining fresh basil leaves and garnish with toasted pine nuts if desired.

{ **VARIATIONS** There are infinite variations to this healthy dish. Mix in cooked or raw vegetables such as chopped celery or peas. Or, add fresh fruit such as chopped mangoes. }

Spaghetti Café Luna

PREP TIME: 2 MINUTES   **COOK TIME:** 10 MINUTES   **SERVES:** 4 TO 5

Often called Pink Pasta, this creamy tomato pasta is a kid favorite. It's the fastest meal you will ever make. By the time the pasta is cooked, the sauce is ready! In fact, this recipe is so good, it has become a cooking favorite of many of our friends.

DID YOU KNOW?

If you burn the garlic while cooking it, you have to start over.

1 pound spaghetti

4 tablespoons olive oil, divided

1 large or 2 medium whole garlic cloves, peeled

1 15-ounce can, good quality plain tomato sauce

¼ teaspoon sea salt

½ cup heavy whipping cream

½ cup freshly grated Parmesan cheese

HELPING HANDS

Young children can stir in the cream. Older ones can prepare the entire dish with supervision.

Bring 4 quarts of water to a boil in a large pot over high heat. When the water is boiling, add 2 tablespoons salt and spaghetti. Reduce heat to medium-high and cook uncovered, according to package directions, stirring occasionally.

Meanwhile, heat 2 tablespoons olive oil in a medium heavy-bottomed saucepan, over low to medium heat. Add garlic and cook for 2 minutes — don't let the garlic burn.

Add tomato sauce and salt. Stir to mix and bring to a boil. Cover, reduce heat to low and simmer for 10 minutes, stirring occasionally. Remove from heat and stir in heavy cream. Taste and adjust for salt.

Drain spaghetti and toss with the sauce, add remaining olive oil. Sprinkle with Parmesan cheese and serve.

Fusilli alla Checca

PREP TIME: 5 MINUTES   **COOK TIME:** 10 MINUTES   **REST TIME:** 30 MINUTES   **SERVES:** 4 TO 5

This is a great summer pasta dish, when fresh juicy tomatoes are abundant! Don't tell anyone about the secret ingredient – anchovies. No one will know, and the recipe won't be the same without them.

KITCHEN TIP:

It is better to tear the basil leaves than to cut them with a knife. The metal causes it to oxidize, which darkens the color and changes the taste.

HELPING HANDS

Young children can help stir the tomatoes and seasonings. Older ones can prepare all ingredients with supervision.

DID YOU KNOW?

Tomatoes are an excellent source of vitamin C, which is most concentrated in the jellylike substance that surrounds the seeds.

1 pound fusilli pasta

6 large red juicy tomatoes, chopped in ½-inch cubes

12 large fresh basil leaves, torn into small pieces

1 garlic clove, peeled and minced

2 tablespoons capers

2 anchovies, cut into very fine pieces

2 tablespoons fresh flat-leaf parsley, rinsed and chopped fine

½ tablespoon fresh oregano, rinsed and chopped fine

¾ cup extra-virgin olive oil

½ teaspoon sea salt

¼ teaspoon freshly ground pepper

Put the tomatoes, basil, garlic, capers, anchovies, parsley, oregano, salt, pepper and olive oil in a large glass serving bowl. Let stand for at least 30 minutes at room temperature so all the flavors can blend.

During the last 20 minutes, bring 4 quarts of water to a boil in a large pot over high heat. When the water is boiling, add 2 tablespoons salt and fusilli pasta. Reduce heat to medium-high and cook uncovered, according to package directions, stirring occasionally.

Drain the pasta and toss with tomato mixture. Taste and adjust for salt and pepper. Eat hot or at room temperature.

Polenta

PREP TIME: 5 MINUTES   **COOK TIME:** 30 MINUTES   **SERVES:** 6

Acknowledged as a healthy dish in the Mediterranean diet, polenta has been a food staple in northern Italy for centuries.

> 3 cups chicken broth, divided
>
> ½ teaspoon salt
>
> 1 cup yellow cornmeal, fine grind
>
> 4 tablespoons butter
>
> ¼ cup freshly grated Parmesan cheese

Pour 2 cups chicken broth into a medium saucepan. Bring to a boil over high heat. Add salt.

Meanwhile, place cornmeal in a small bowl with remaining chicken broth. When broth is boiling add "wet cornmeal" and all excess liquid, stirring constantly with a wire whisk. Reduce heat to medium and continue stirring with a wooden spoon for about 25 to 30 minutes until done.

DID YOU KNOW?

Corn was brought to Italy from the Americas by European explorers.

HELPING HANDS

Young children can help measure the cornmeal.

KITCHEN TIP:

Mixing the cornmeal with some liquid makes it easier to stir into the boiling broth.

{ **VARIATIONS** You can also use water instead of the chicken broth and adjust for salt. }

Risotto

PREP TIME: 5 MINUTES **COOK TIME:** 25 MINUTES **SERVES:** 6

Properly cooked risotto has a creamy consistency yet each individual rice grain remains "al dente." Some chefs say not to stir the risotto to prevent the grains from breaking, but our mothers always stirred it so the starch in the rice would mix with the broth and make it creamy.

5 cups chicken broth

4 tablespoons butter, divided

½ small onion, peeled and chopped very fine, about ½ cup

I pound Arborio or Carnaroli rice, about 2¼ cups

¼ cup dry white wine

½ cup freshly grated Parmesan cheese

DID YOU KNOW?

Arborio and Carnaroli are short grain varieties that get creamy as they absorb the flavorful broth.

Heat broth in a medium saucepan over low heat.

Melt 2 tablespoons butter in a large saucepan over low to medium heat. Add onion and sauté until it becomes translucent, 2 to 3 minutes.

Add rice and sauté until each grain is coated with the butter, stirring constantly so rice does not burn. You will hear soft, popping noises as the rice begins to toast.

After 2 minutes, add wine and stir until liquid has evaporated.

HELPING HANDS

Young children can help measure the rice.

Add warm broth to rice about 1 large ladleful at a time – stirring after each addition. Allow liquid to evaporate, then add another ladleful, (about 1 cup) of broth. Repeat.

When rice is tender but not mushy, after 18 to 20 minutes, remove from heat and stir in remaining 2 tablespoons butter and Parmesan cheese. Serve immediately.

Risotto Cakes or Timbale

Butter a 6-cup ring mold, or six 1-cup molds, or 12 foil muffin cups. Remove risotto from stove after 15 minutes of cooking time. Stir in remaining 2 tablespoons butter and Parmesan cheese. Spoon risotto into prepared mold. (Can be prepared ahead of time to this point and kept in the refrigerator, covered with plastic wrap.) Bake uncovered at 350°F for 10 minutes. Let rest 5 minutes, then invert onto a large plate.

Simple Tomato Sauce

PREP TIME: 5 MINUTES **COOK TIME:** 35 MINUTES **MAKES:** 4 CUPS

This tomato sauce is very easy to make. The classic combination of sautéed onions, carrots and celery is the base to many Italian recipes. This mixture in Italian is called "soffritto."

¼ cup olive oil

½ onion, peeled and chopped fine, about ½ cup

I small carrot, peeled and chopped fine

I celery rib, rinsed and chopped fine

2 I5-ounce cans, good quality tomato sauce

½ teaspoon sea salt

Dash freshly ground pepper

6 fresh basil leaves, rinsed and dried

½ cup freshly grated Parmesan cheese

DID YOU KNOW?
Blending the sauce gives it a creamy consistency and hides the vegetables from picky eaters.

HELPING HANDS
Young children can rinse the vegetables, older ones can peel them.

KITCHEN TIP:
Add the basil at the end so the heat does not spoil the flavor.

Heat olive oil in a medium skillet over low to medium heat. Add onion, carrot and celery. Sauté for 5 minutes, stirring occasionally.

Add tomato sauce and salt. Bring to a boil. Cover, reduce heat to low and simmer for 20 minutes, stirring occasionally. Remove from heat.

Taste sauce and adjust for salt and pepper. Remove from heat and stir in basil leaves. Let sit for 10 minutes so the sauce absorbs the basil flavor.

Remove the basil and blend the sauce with an immersion blender or in a standard blender in small batches. *(Be careful when blending hot liquids!)*

Spaghetti with Simple Tomato Sauce

PREP TIME: 5 MINUTES   **COOK TIME:** 10 MINUTES   **SERVES:** 4 TO 5

In general, choose a pasta shape and sauce that complement each other. Angel hair or thin spaghetti should be served with light sauces. Thicker pasta shapes, like fettuccine, work well with heavier sauces and pasta shapes with holes or ridges are perfect for chunky sauces.

1 pound spaghetti

2 cups Simple Tomato Sauce, pg 110

2 tablespoons extra-virgin olive oil

1/2 cup freshly grated Parmesan cheese

Bring 4 quarts of water to boil in a large pot over high heat. When the water is boiling, add 2 tablespoons salt and pasta. Reduce heat to medium-high and cook uncovered, according to package directions, stirring occasionally.

Meanwhile, in a small sauce pan warm up sauce over low heat. When pasta is cooked, drain and pour into a large serving bowl. Toss with warm sauce and olive oil. Sprinkle with Parmesan cheese.

HELPING HANDS

Young children can select their favorite pasta shape. Older ones can grate the cheese.

KITCHEN TIP:

Use leftover sauce as a dip for soft breadsticks or fried mozzarella cheese sticks.

Penne con Scampi

PREP TIME: 5 MINUTES   **COOK TIME:** 30 MINUTES   **SERVES:** 4 TO 5

This is another typical recipe of Versilia, the Italian Riviera where Rima is from.

1 pound penne pasta

2 tablespoons salt

2 tablespoons olive oil

1 tablespoon butter

½ onion, peeled and chopped fine, about ½ cup

3 garlic cloves, peeled and minced

½ teaspoon red pepper flakes

3 tablespoons chopped flat-leaf parsley

2 tablespoons brandy

1 pound medium, raw shrimp, peeled and deveined

½ teaspoon sea salt

Dash freshly ground pepper

1 15-ounce can, good quality plain tomato sauce

½ cup heavy whipping cream

KITCHEN TIP:

It's best to use fresh medium-size shrimp, but uncooked and frozen 21/30 count per pound, will do.

DID YOU KNOW?

The dish will be more flavorful if you finish cooking the pasta in the prepared sauce.

Heat olive oil and butter in a large 12-inch skillet over low to medium heat. Add onion and sauté until translucent, about 5 minutes. Add garlic and pepper flakes, cook for 2 minutes, then add parsley and cook for 1 more minute. Add brandy – *be careful when adding the brandy to the pan, it could catch fire.* The alcohol will "burn off," leaving behind a great flavor. Raise the heat and cook until half the liquid evaporates.

Add shrimp and let cook for 3 to 4 minutes, turning them after 2 minutes. Season with salt and pepper. Remove shrimp and set aside. Add tomato sauce. Bring to a boil. Reduce heat to low, cover and simmer for 20 minutes.

Stir in cream. Simmer for 2 minutes, then remove from heat and add the cooked shrimp.

Meanwhile, bring 4 quarts of water to a boil in a large pot over high heat. When the water is boiling, add 2 tablespoons of salt and penne pasta. Reduce heat to medium-high and cook uncovered, stirring occasionally.

When penne are 3 minutes from being done, transfer them to the sauce in the skillet using a slotted spoon. Add about ½ cup of the cooking water and cook for a few minutes over medium heat, stirring often and adding more water if necessary. The pasta will finish cooking in the sauce. Taste and adjust for salt, pepper flakes and cream. Serve immediately.

Gnocchi

PREP TIME: 2 HOURS 30 MINUTES **COOK TIME:** 10 MINUTES **SERVES:** 6

Gnocchi is the Italian name for a dumpling usually made with potato and flour. Making them is straightforward, but the best results are achieved with a little practice.

3 large russet potatoes, about 2 pounds

1 large egg

1 tablespoon extra-virgin olive oil

1 teaspoon sea salt

1 cup all-purpose flour

Additional flour for dusting

DID YOU KNOW?

To freeze, place fresh gnocchi on a baking sheet and freeze for 30 minutes. Transfer to a resealable plastic bag and freeze.

Bake the potatoes at 400°F for 1 hour. Allow to cool, about one hour. Remove skins and discard.

Place a mixing bowl on a scale and set to zero. Keep the bowl on the scale! Pass potatoes through a ricer and allow them to fall into the mixing bowl. Continue ricing potatoes until you have 1 pound, about 4 cups.

HELPING HANDS

Young children can help rice the potatoes and make the gnocchi.

Remove bowl from scale and mix in egg, olive oil and salt with a fork. Place mixing bowl back on scale and set to zero. Slowly, add flour until you have added 6 ounces, about 1 cup.

Remove mixing bowl from scale and mix in flour with a fork until just combined. Incorporate well without overworking the mixture! Form into a ball and turn out onto a lightly floured surface.

KITCHEN TIP:

For light and pillow-soft gnocchi, use a kitchen scale to measure the ingredients.

Divide dough into 4 equal pieces. Roll each piece into a rope about ¾ inch in diameter. Set aside. Continue in this manner until all the dough is rolled into ropes. Cut ropes into ½ inch pieces. Roll each piece against a fork, or the back of a cheese grater, using your thumb to make an indentation. Lightly flour your thumb and utensil of choice as you roll each piece of dough. Place gnocchi on a baking sheet that has been lightly sprinkled with flour. Continue until all gnocchi are made.

COOK THE GNOCCHI:

Bring 4 quarts of water to boil in a large pot over high heat. When the water is boiling, add 2 tablespoons salt. Place about 20 gnocchi in the boiling salted water. Gnocchi cook in about one or two minutes. Remove from the water with a slotted strainer as soon as they float to the top. Place immediately in a heated serving bowl and cover with a little warm sauce or melted butter.

Gnocchi with Tomato Meat Ragu

COOK TIME: 10 MINUTES **SERVES:** 6

Claudia learned to make gnocchi from her grandmother. She would cover the finished dish and let it sit for 10 minutes in a warm oven to give the gnocchi a chance to absorb the flavors from the delicious sauce.

HELPING HANDS
Young children can help spoon the Tomato Meat Ragu over the gnocchi.

1 batch gnocchi, pg 114 OR 1 pound store-bought gnocchi

2 cups Tomato Meat Ragu, pg 96, warmed

2 tablespoons olive oil

½ cup freshly grated Parmesan cheese

Bring 4 quarts of water to boil in a large pot over high heat.

Meanwhile, in a medium saucepan warm the Tomato Meat Ragu with the olive oil over low heat, stirring occasionally.

When the water is boiling, add 2 tablespoons salt. Place about 20 gnocchi in the boiling salted water. Gnocchi cook in about one or two minutes. Remove them from the water with a slotted strainer as soon as they float to the top. Place immediately in a heated serving bowl and cover with a little Tomato Meat Ragu.

Repeat with remaining gnocchi and sauce. Sprinkle with freshly grated Parmesan cheese.

Baked Gnocchi

COOK TIME: 25 MINUTES   **SERVES:** 6

Gnocchi can be made in different colors by adding a tablespoon of tomato paste, pureed spinach or pureed carrots to the flour before mixing the dough.

1 batch gnocchi, pg 114 OR 1 pound store-bought gnocchi

4 tablespoons butter, divided

½ cup half and half

2 ounces fontina cheese, grated

2 ounces blue cheese, crumbled

2 ounces mozzarella cheese, shredded

Dash freshly ground pepper

½ cup freshly grated Parmesan cheese

HELPING HANDS

Young children can help select their favorite cheese.

KITCHEN TIP:

You can purchase ready-made gnocchi, but they will not taste as good.

Preheat oven to 350°F. Grease a 9 x 9-inch oven-proof baking dish.

Melt butter in a medium saucepan over low heat. Add half and half, fontina, blue and mozzarella cheeses. Stir gently until all the cheeses have melted. Stir in pepper. Pour half the sauce into a prepared dish. Set remainder aside.

Meanwhile, bring 4 quarts of water to boil in a large pot over high heat. When the water is boiling, add 2 tablespoons salt. Place about 20 gnocchi in the boiling salted water. Gnocchi cook in about one or two minutes. Remove them from the water with a slotted strainer as soon as they float to the top. Place immediately in the baking dish and cover with a little more cheese sauce. Repeat with remaining gnocchi and sauce.

Sprinkle with freshly grated Parmesan cheese. Bake for 15 minutes or until the top browns slightly. Remove from the oven and let rest for 5 minutes.

{ **VARIATIONS** Try your own mixture of favorite cheeses. }

Pesto

PREP TIME: 20 MINUTES   **DRYING TIME:** 30 TO 60 MINUTES   **MAKES:** 1½ CUPS

Pesto is a brilliant green fresh basil sauce that comes from the Liguria region of Italy.

3 cups fresh basil, about 2 to 3 ounces, leaves only

¼ teaspoon sea salt

I garlic clove, peeled

½ cup grated Parmesan cheese

I ounce pine nuts, about 2 tablespoons

I cup extra-virgin olive oil

Remove basil leaves from stems, rinse and dry completely.

Place basil, salt, garlic, Parmesan cheese, pine nuts and ½ cup olive oil in a blender, blend for a few seconds. Remove lid and push down basil leaves with a wooden spoon or rubber scraper.

Slowly add the remaining olive oil, while the blender is running on low speed, blending until the pesto is completely smooth, about 3 to 5 minutes. Taste and adjust for salt.

Use immediately or store in the refrigerator, covered with extra-virgin olive oil or in small portions in the freezer for up to 2 months.

Spaghetti al Pesto

PREP TIME: 10 MINUTES   **COOK TIME:** 10 MINUTES   **SERVES:** 4 TO 5

I pound spaghetti

I cup pesto, see above

¼ to ½ cup extra-virgin olive oil

½ cup freshly grated Parmesan cheese

Bring 4 quarts of water to a boil in a large pot. When the water is boiling, add 2 tablespoons salt and spaghetti. Reduce heat to medium-high and cook uncovered, according to package directions, stirring occasionally.

Put pesto in a large serving bowl, add olive oil and stir. Add ¼ cup of the pasta cooking water and stir. Drain the pasta, add to sauce, mix well, taste and adjust for salt. Sprinkle with Parmesan cheese. Serve immediately.

Lentils & Rice with Caramelized Red Onions

PREP TIME: 10 MINUTES **COOK TIME:** 60 MINUTES **SERVES:** 4

The dense texture of lentils pairs well with the fluffy rice. The caramelized red onions look pretty and provide a tasty accent. Reserve a large spoonful of them for garnish.

1/4 cup olive oil

2 red onions, peeled and sliced thin, half-moon shape

2 cup lentils, rinsed

1 teaspoon salt

1 cup uncooked rice

Heat olive oil in a medium saucepan over low heat. Add onions. To caramelize, cook over low to medium heat for 15 minutes, stirring occasionally. When done, remove one fourth of the onions to a plate and set aside.

To the same saucepan, add 6 cups water, lentils and salt. Reduce heat to low, cover and simmer for 30 minutes. Stir in rice, cover and simmer for 20 more minutes. Remove from heat. Taste and adjust for salt. Garnish with remaining caramelized onions.

DID YOU KNOW?

Lentils are good for you and easy to prepare. Lentils contain a large amount of fiber. Studies show that eating lentils or beans two or more times a week reduces the risk of breast cancer.

HELPING HANDS

Young children can help measure the lentils and rice.

CURIOSITY:

Italian folklore suggests eating lentils or lentil soup on New Year's Day to bring good luck and prosperity in the coming year.

Spaghetti Carbonara

PREP TIME: 5 MINUTES   **COOK TIME:** 10 MINUTES   **SERVES:** 4 TO 5

This is a quick and easy pasta dish. Most of the ingredients are already in your pantry!

- 1 pound spaghetti
- 4 ounces pancetta, cut into ¼-inch cubes OR 4 slices cooked bacon or ham, cut into small pieces
- 3 large eggs
- ¼ cup butter, cut into fourths
- 1 cup freshly grated Parmesan cheese, divided

HELPING HANDS

Young children can help beat the eggs. Older ones can cut the pancetta.

KITCHEN TIP

The heat of the pasta will "cook" the eggs and melt the butter and cheese.

Cook the pancetta in a nonstick small skillet over low heat, stirring occasionally. When pancetta is done, after about 8 minutes, drain on a plate covered with a paper towel.

Meanwhile, bring 4 quarts of water to a boil in a large pot over high heat. When the water is boiling, add 2 tablespoons salt and spaghetti. Reduce heat to medium-high and cook uncovered, according to package directions, stirring occasionally.

Place eggs in a medium bowl and beat well. Drain the pasta, reserving some of the cooking water. Return pasta to the cooking pot and add the beaten eggs. Stir briskly. Add the pancetta, butter and ½ cup Parmesan cheese. Continue stirring until the cheese has melted. Add some cooking water if the sauce seems too thick. Sprinkle with remaining Parmesan cheese. Serve immediately.

Penne al Forno

PREP TIME: 20 MINUTES   **COOK TIME:** 3 HOURS   **SERVES:** 8 TO 10

This is a very traditional recipe from Rima's family. It is prepared for many parties and is loved by everyone.

1 pound penne pasta

½ cup olive oil

4 pounds yellow onions, peeled and thinly sliced in half-moons

5 garlic cloves, peeled

4 cups chicken broth

2 teaspoons sea salt

¼ teaspoon freshly ground pepper

4 cups Béchamel White Sauce, pg 97

1 cup freshly grated Parmesan cheese

DID YOU KNOW?

Onions are rich in powerful sulfur-containing compounds that are responsible for their health-promoting benefits.

KITCHEN TIP:

Leave a corner of the mixture without onions. Some kids love the flavor but not the sight of onions in their pasta.

Heat olive oil in a large pot over low heat. Add the onions and garlic. Cook for 20 to 25 minutes, stirring often. Add chicken broth, salt and pepper. Cover and let cook for 1½ hours.

During the last 20 minutes, start cooking the penne. Bring 4 quarts of water to a boil in a large pot over high heat. When the water is boiling, add 2 tablespoons of salt and penne. Reduce heat to medium-high, cook, stirring occasionally.

Heat oven to 350°F.

Drain the pasta a few minutes before it is done. (It will continue cooking in the oven.) Transfer to a large 9 x 13-inch baking dish or individual ramekins.

Stir in the onion mixture and half the Béchamel White Sauce until well mixed. Spread the remaining Béchamel on top and sprinkle with Parmesan cheese.

Bake for 40 minutes. Broil for 3 to 4 minutes or until top is golden brown. Let rest for 10 minutes before serving.

Risotto Milanese

PREP TIME: 5 MINUTES   **COOK TIME:** 25 MINUTES   **SERVES:** 6 TO 8

The addition of saffron to this traditional recipe of the Milano Italy area produces a beautiful golden and aromatic dish.

5 cups chicken broth

4 tablespoons butter, divided

½ small onion, peeled and chopped very fine, about ½ cup

I pound Arborio or Carnaroli rice, about 2¼ cups

¼ cup dry white wine

½ teaspoon saffron threads

½ cup freshly grated Parmesan cheese, plus additional for serving

Heat broth, salt and saffron threads in a medium saucepan over low heat. Stir to dissolve saffron.

Melt 2 tablespoons butter in a large saucepan over low to medium heat. Add onions and sauté until they become translucent, 2 to 3 minutes.

Add rice and sauté until each grain is coated with butter, stirring constantly so rice does not burn. You will hear soft, popping noises as the rice begins to toast.

After 2 minutes, add wine and stir until liquid has evaporated.

Add saffron broth to rice about 1 large ladleful at a time – stirring after each addition. Allow liquid to evaporate, then add another ladleful, about 1 cup of broth. Repeat.

When rice is tender but not mushy, in about 18 to 20 minutes, remove from heat and stir in remaining 2 tablespoons butter and Parmesan cheese. Serve immediately with additional Parmesan cheese.

Spaghetti with Clams

PREP TIME: 10 MINUTES   **COOK TIME:** 30 MINUTES   **SERVES:** 4 TO 5

Pasta with clams is a popular restaurant dish in the U.S. and in Italy. With thousands of miles of coastline, Italians eagerly enjoy clams in a variety of ways.

KITCHEN TIP:

To make steamed clams, follow the directions for preparing the clams up to "remove from heat."

DID YOU KNOW?

Fresh clams should be tightly closed and should not smell. Throw away clams that do not open after cooking!

FOR THE PASTA & SAUCE:

1 pound spaghetti

½ cup olive oil

4 garlic cloves, peeled

1 dried red pepper OR ¼ to ½ teaspoon red pepper flakes

¼ cup flat-leaf parsley, rinsed and chopped fine

½ cup dry white wine

½ teaspoon sea salt

FOR THE CLAMS:

5 pounds clams, rinsed and drained

¼ cup olive oil

4 garlic cloves, peeled

2 tablespoons flat-leaf parsley, rinsed and chopped fine

2 tablespoons dry white wine

PREPARE THE CLAMS:

Heat olive oil in a large saucepan over medium heat. Add garlic, clams, parsley and wine. Cover and simmer for 5 minutes, shaking the pot occasionally. Remove from heat. Shell most of the clams, keeping some whole for garnish. Pass the cooking liquid through a fine sieve and reserve.

PREPARE THE SAUCE:

Heat olive oil in a large sauté pan over medium heat. Add garlic, red pepper, remaining parsley and clam meat. Sauté for 2 minutes, add wine and let it evaporate. Add salt and reserved clam cooking liquid. Reduce heat to low and simmer for 2 minutes.

PREPARE THE PASTA:

Meanwhile, bring 4 quarts of water to boil in a large pot over high heat. When the water is boiling, add 2 tablespoons salt and spaghetti. Reduce heat to medium-high and cook uncovered, stirring occasionally.

When spaghetti are 3 minutes from being done, using tongs or a pasta server, transfer them to the clam sauce in the sauté pan. Add a little of the cooking water and cook for a few minutes over medium heat, stirring often. The pasta will finish cooking in the sauce. Garnish with reserved whole clams. Serve.

Penne with Asparagus

PREP TIME: 5 MINUTES   **COOK TIME:** 20 MINUTES   **SERVES:** 4 TO 5

We dedicate this recipe to the fertile San Joaquin Valley where asparagus is king!

I pound penne rigate

¼ cup olive oil

I onion, peeled and chopped fine, about I cup

2 pounds asparagus, rinsed and cut into ½-inch pieces

¼ teaspoon sea salt

Dash freshly ground pepper

I cup heavy whipping cream

½ cup freshly grated Parmesan cheese, divided

Heat the olive oil in a large skillet over low to medium heat. Add onion and sauté until translucent, about 5 to 8 minutes.

Meanwhile, bring 4 quarts of water to a boil in a large pot over high heat. When the water is boiling, add 2 tablespoons of salt and penne pasta. Reduce heat to medium-high and cook, uncovered, stirring occasionally.

Add the asparagus, salt and pepper to the onions. Continue cooking, stirring occasionally. After 5 minutes, add cream and cook for 2 more minutes.

Meanwhile, pour hot water into a serving bowl and let stand. This is an important step which serves to warm the bowl.

When penne are 3 minutes from being done, transfer them to the sauce in the skillet using a slotted spoon. Add about ½ cup of the cooking water and cook for a few minutes over medium heat, stirring often and adding more water if necessary. The pasta will finish cooking in the sauce. Taste and adjust for salt and pepper. Stir in ¼ cup Parmesan cheese.

When the penne are ready, pour out the water and dry the serving bowl. Transfer penne to the bowl. Sprinkle with remaining Parmesan cheese and serve.

{ **VARIATIONS** For added flavor, stir in ½ cup cooked and chopped pancetta just before serving. }

Farfalle Caprese

PREP TIME: 10 MINUTES **COOK TIME:** 10 MINUTES **REST TIME:** 60 MINUTES **SERVES:** 4 TO 5

Bowtie or butterfly pasta have the perfect shape to pair with bite-size pieces of tomatoes and mozzarella cheese.

I pound butterfly (bowtie) pasta

8 ounces fresh mozzarella, cut into ½-inch dice

4 medium size tomatoes, the best you can find, cut in ½-inch dice
OR I pint colorful baby tomatoes, rinsed and cut in half

8 fresh basil leaves, torn into small pieces

½ cup extra-virgin olive oil

½ teaspoon sea salt

Dash freshly ground pepper

Stir together the mozzarella, tomatoes, basil, olive oil, salt and pepper in a large serving bowl. Let rest at room temperature for about 1 hour.

Bring 4 quarts of water to boil in a large pot over high heat. When the water is boiling, add 2 tablespoons salt and bow-tie pasta. Reduce heat to medium-high and cook uncovered, according to package directions, stirring occasionally.

Drain the bow-tie pasta and add it to the tomato mixture. Toss well. Taste and adjust for salt, pepper and olive oil. Cover, let sit for 2 minutes, then serve.

CUROSITY:
The origin of mozzarella cheese is linked to southern Italy where it was originally produced from water buffalo milk.

HELPING HANDS
Young children can help tear the basil leaves. Older ones can cut the mozzarella and the tomatoes with supervision.

KITCHEN TIP:
The longer you marinate the tomatoes and mozzarella, the better the flavor.

Fettuccine with Peas

PREP TIME: 5 MINUTES **COOK TIME:** 20 MINUTES **SERVES:** 4 TO 5

When Rima made this dish with spinach pasta, Shane, a family friend refused to eat it because he said that he did not like spinach. She bet him that he would not be able to tell the difference if he were blind-folded. He accepted the challenge, and of course he lost! He loved it and now it is one of his favorite pasta dishes.

I pound fettuccine pasta

2 tablespoons butter

¼ onion, peeled and chopped fine, about ¼ cup

10 ounces peas, fresh or frozen

½ cup chicken broth

Pinch sea salt

Dash freshly ground pepper

½ cup heavy whipping cream

I cup freshly grated Parmesan cheese, divided

Bring 4 quarts of water to boil in a large pot over high heat. When the water is boiling, add 2 tablespoons salt and fettuccine. Reduce heat to medium-high and cook, uncovered, according to package directions, stirring occasionally.

Meanwhile, melt butter in a medium skillet over low heat. Add onion and sauté over low to medium heat for 5 minutes. Add the peas and cook for 5 minutes. Add chicken broth, salt and pepper, and cook for 5 more minutes. Add cream, bring to a boil while stirring. Remove from heat. Stir in ½ cup of Parmesan cheese.

Meanwhile, pour hot water into a serving bowl and let stand. This is an important step which serves to warm the bowl.

When the fettuccine are ready, pour out the water and dry the serving bowl. Pour the sauce into the serving bowl, drain the cooked fettuccine, add to the bowl and toss with the sauce. Sprinkle with remaining Parmesan cheese. Serve immediately.

White Rice

COOK TIME: 20 MINUTES **SERVES:** 2 TO 3

Rice is a staple food for many of the world's populations. Over 50 varieties are grown in Italy. Riso in bianco is simply steamed rice.

> 2 cups water
>
> I teaspoon salt
>
> I cup long-grain rice

Place water in a medium saucepan. Bring to a boil over high heat. Add salt and rice and stir. Cover, reduce heat to low and cook for 20 minutes. Do not lift the lid to peek.

Turn off heat and stir with a fork to fluff and separate the grains.

HELPING HANDS
Young children can help "fluff" the rice after it has steamed.

DID YOU KNOW?
Rice is low in fat and calories while high in nutrients.

Basmati Rice

COOK TIME: 20 MINUTES **SERVES:** 2 TO 3

Basmati rice is an aromatic, long-grain rice with a sweet taste that has been used in India and Pakistan for thousands of years. Several varieties are now grown in the U.S. and are increasing in popularity.

> I½ cups water
>
> I cup Basmati rice
>
> ½ teaspoon salt

Place water in a medium saucepan. Bring to a boil over high heat. Add salt and rice and stir. Cover, reduce heat to low and cook for 15 minutes. Do not lift the lid to peek.

Turn off heat and let rest for 5 minutes. Stir with a fork to fluff and separate the grains.

CURIOSITY:
The Hindi word 'basmati' means fragrant.

HELPING HANDS
Older children can make the dish with supervision.

meat
poultry AND seafood

WE KNOW that if we do not prepare meals for our families, then someone else will. Cooking at home allows us to choose wholesome ingredients that provide the best nutrition possible.

Arrosto

PREP TIME: 10 MINUTES   **COOK TIME:** 45 TO 60 MINUTES   **REST TIME:** 15 MINUTES   **SERVES:** 4 TO 6

This is what you make for dinner when you have 45 minutes and a hungry crew. With very little effort, you can make everybody happy.

1 eye of round roast, 4 to 5 pounds

8 garlic cloves, peeled

4 small sprigs fresh rosemary, cut in half

2 tablespoons sea salt, divided

1 tablespoon freshly ground pepper, divided

½ cup olive oil, divided

2 pounds new potatoes, rinsed

Preheat oven to 400°F.

Place potatoes in a large roasting pan. Sprinkle with ½ tablespoon sea salt and ¼ tablespoon pepper. Drizzle evenly with ¼ cup olive oil. Mix well so each potato is coated with oil.

With a paring knife, stab the roast and spin the knife to create a small hole. Using your fingers, stuff each hole with 1 clove of garlic, ½ sprig rosemary, ⅛ teaspoon salt and ⅛ teaspoon pepper. Do this in 8 different places on the roast.

Place the meat in a roasting pan with potatoes, rub with remaining salt and pepper. Drizzle with olive oil and bake for 45 to 60 minutes – turning the roast every 20 minutes. If the bottom of the pan looks dry, add a little olive oil.

When internal temperature measures 145°F for medium-rare, remove roast from oven, place on a cutting board with a liquid moat, and tent with aluminum foil. Let rest for 15 minutes. Place pan back in the oven and let potatoes cook while roast is resting. Carve roast into thin slices and serve with cooking juices and potatoes.

DID YOU KNOW?

This roast is also excellent the next day – thinly sliced and seasoned with extra-virgin olive oil, salt, pepper and a couple of drops of lemon juice.

HELPING HANDS

Young children can help peel the garlic. Older ones can prepare the roast.

KITCHEN TIP:

You can also cook this roast in a large pan on the stove. Sear on all sides in olive oil. Cover, then cook over low heat for about 45 minutes, turning occasionally.

Chicken Cacciatora

PREP TIME: 10 MINUTES **COOK TIME:** 60 MINUTES **SERVES:** 4 TO 6

This dish is typical of the Tuscan tradition. It is very easy to prepare. The garlic and rosemary improve the flavor of the chicken and the tomato sauce helps to tenderize it. Let the tempting aromas of these fragrant ingredients fill your home with the promise of a great family meal.

1 pound package chicken drumsticks

1 pound package chicken thighs

4 tablespoons olive oil

4 garlic cloves, peeled

4 small sprigs fresh rosemary

1 teaspoon sea salt

Dash freshly ground pepper

1 15-ounce can good quality tomato sauce

¼ cup olives

Rinse chicken pieces and pat dry with paper towel. Set aside.

Heat olive oil in a large heavy-bottomed pan over medium heat. Add garlic cloves and 2 sprigs of rosemary and sauté for 2 minutes. Add chicken pieces and continue cooking and stirring until brown on all sides, about 10 minutes.

Season with salt and pepper. Add tomato sauce, ½ cup water and remaining 2 sprigs of rosemary. Cover, reduce heat to very low and simmer for 45 minutes, stirring occasionally.

Add olives and simmer for 5 minutes more. Remove from heat and serve with polenta, rice or pasta.

Chicken Pizzaiola

PREP TIME: 10 MINUTES   **COOK TIME:** 15 MINUTES   **SERVES:** 4

"Pizzaiola" is Italian for anything cooked with tomato and mozzarella. Quick-cooking chicken cutlets are the perfect beginning for this dish.

1 pound boneless, skinless chicken breast fillets, pg 253

1 large egg

½ teaspoon sea salt

⅛ teaspoon freshly ground pepper

1 cup bread crumbs

4 tablespoons olive oil, divided

1 8-ounce fresh mozzarella ball, sliced

1 cup Simple Tomato Sauce, pg 110

HELPING HANDS
Young children can help place the tomato sauce and the cheese on cutlets. Older ones can make the dish with supervision.

Beat egg in a small bowl with a fork. Add salt and pepper. Place chicken in egg mixture and mix so all pieces become coated.

Place bread crumbs on a large plate. Dip each chicken piece into the breadcrumbs. Turn to coat both sides, patting gently to remove excess crumbs. Place on a separate plate. Repeat until all chicken is coated.

Heat 2 tablespoons olive oil in a large non-stick skillet, over medium heat. When oil is hot, place a few breaded pieces in the pan and cook for 2 to 3 minutes, or when the edges turn light beige. Turn and cook for 3 minutes more, or until thoroughly cooked. Transfer to a large baking dish. Repeat with remaining olive oil and chicken pieces.

Place 2 tablespoons tomato sauce and a slice of mozzarella cheese on each piece of chicken. Bake at 350°F for 5 minutes or until cheese melts. Serve immediately.

Almond Baked Halibut

PREP TIME: 10 MINUTES **COOK TIME:** 15 MINUTES **SERVES:** 4

Eating fish is a healthy alternative. This simple preparation means dinner is ready in minutes!

FOR THE HALIBUT:

1½ pounds halibut fillets

4 tablespoons olive oil, divided

½ cup almond meal (finely ground almonds)

½ teaspoon sea salt

Freshly ground pepper

FOR THE LEEKS:

¼ cup olive oil

2 leeks, rinsed well and sliced thin

1 large onion, peeled and sliced thin

¼ teaspoon sea salt

¼ cup dry white wine

DID YOU KNOW?

Halibut is a nutrient-dense food. It is a good source of high quality protein and omega-3 essential fatty acids.

HELPING HANDS

Young children can help dip the halibut in the ground almonds. Older ones can chop the leeks and onions with supervision.

KITCHEN TIP

For a lighter version, cook the leeks in chicken broth instead of olive oil.

Preheat oven to 400°F.

Pour 2 tablespoons olive oil in a 9 x 13-inch baking dish.

Place almond meal on a small plate. Dip one side of the halibut in the almond meal and pat gently to remove any excess. Place in the baking dish, almond side up. Sprinkle with salt and pepper. Drizzle with remaining 2 tablespoons olive oil. Bake for 12 to 15 minutes, or until done.

Meanwhile, heat ¼ cup olive oil in a large, heavy bottom skillet over low heat. Add leeks and onions, sprinkle with sea salt. Cover and cook for 8 to 15 minutes, stirring occasionally. Leeks should turn a light brown but not burn! Add white wine, increase heat and cook for 1 minute until liquid has evaporated. Remove from heat. Serve with halibut.

Lamb Chops

PREP TIME: 10 MINUTES **MARINATE:** 2 HOURS **COOK TIME:** 15 MINUTES **SERVES:** 4

Lamb chops are a good choice for a simple family meal. These grilled chops are tasty and easy to prepare.

¾ cup olive oil

¼ cup red wine vinegar

Juice of one lemon

4 garlic cloves, peeled and minced

2 small sprigs fresh rosemary

8 lamb chops, about 4 ounces each

½ teaspoon sea salt

¼ teaspoon freshly ground pepper

DID YOU KNOW?

Sheep are the most abundant livestock in the world. Raised for food and wool, they were originally domesticated in the Middle East and Asia.

HELPING HANDS

Young children can help stir the marinade. Older ones can make the marinade.

Combine olive oil, vinegar, lemon, rosemary and garlic in a small bowl. Pour the marinade into a resealable plastic bag. Add the lamb chops. Seal and refrigerate for at least 2 hours.

Preheat grill to medium high.

Remove lamb chops from marinade and season with salt and pepper. Grill about 7 minutes per side for medium done. Serve warm.

DID YOU KNOW?

Rosemary extract has a long history of medicinal uses for stomach upset, digestive disorders and headaches.

Brasato with Red Wine

PREP TIME: 20 MINUTES **MARINATE:** 12 HOURS **COOK TIME:** 2 HOURS 30 MINUTES **SERVES:** 6

This delicious Sunday night cold-weather recipe was given to us by our Italian friend and great chef, Elena Spadoni. After several hours of simmering in a savory bath, the meat is cut-like-butter tender and very flavorful.

DID YOU KNOW?

Braising means to sear a large piece of meat, then cook it in liquid for a long period of time. Marinating meat gives it more flavor and tenderizes it at the same time.

KITCHEN TIP:

The secret is to throw away the marinade and begin with a new bottle of wine to finish cooking the meat.

1 3-pound top sirloin roast

2 onions, peeled and cut into 8 pieces

6 carrots, peeled and chopped into 8 pieces

4 celery ribs, rinsed and chopped into 8 pieces

4 garlic cloves, peeled

4 small sprigs fresh rosemary

4 whole bay leaves

4 sprigs fresh thyme

4 sprigs fresh oregano

6 whole cloves

2 750ml bottles Cabernet Sauvignon, good quality

¼ cup olive oil

1 tablespoon sea salt

¼ teaspoon freshly ground pepper

2 cups chicken broth

THE NIGHT BEFORE:

Place the beef, half the vegetables and half the herbs in a large resealable plastic bag. Pour contents of 1 bottle of wine into the bag – making sure the meat is completely covered. Seal, place in the refrigerator, and marinate overnight.

The next day, remove the meat and set it aside. Discard the marinade including the vegetables and herbs.

Heat olive oil in a large 6-quart pot over medium heat. Salt and pepper the beef on all sides. Add to pot. Sear on all sides, about 10 minutes, then remove and set aside.

Add the remaining fresh onion, carrots and celery along with the fresh garlic cloves to the same pot and cook over medium heat, stirring often. Cook for 5 to 10 minutes so the oil can absorb the flavors of the vegetables. Then add the beef and the remaining fresh herbs and cloves. Cook for 2 to 3 minutes, and then add the wine and broth.

Bring to a boil, stirring often, reduce heat to low, cover and simmer for 2 to 3 hours. The meat is cooked when it is very tender and falls apart at the touch of a fork. Place the meat on a cutting board and slice into thick slices then transfer to a serving plate. Place the vegetables and the cooking liquid in a blender and mix. *(Be careful when blending hot liquids!)* Pour sauce over meat and serve warm.

Veal Cutlet Milanese

PREP TIME: 10 MINUTES   **COOK TIME:** 10 MINUTES   **SERVES:** 4

For centuries the Italians and the Austrians have been fighting over the origin of this dish. The story says that the emperor of Austria, Franz Joseph, ate it first in Italy at the court of Count Attems. He loved it, was given the recipe and it became his favorite, and soon after the national dish of Austria.

DID YOU KNOW?

In Austria this dish is called Wienerschnitzel.

1 pound veal scaloppine or veal chops, 4 to 6 pieces

1 large egg

½ teaspoon sea salt

⅛ teaspoon freshly ground pepper

1 cup bread crumbs

4 tablespoons olive oil, divided

1 lemon, sliced into 4 wedges, optional

HELPING HANDS

Children can help beat the egg, pound the veal, soak it in the egg mixture or dip it in the breadcrumbs.

Veal scaloppine are usually the proper thickness. Veal chops are thicker and need to be pounded with a meat tenderizer until they are ¼-inch thick.

Beat egg in a small bowl with a fork. Add salt and pepper. Place veal in egg mixture and mix so all pieces become coated.

Place bread crumbs on a large plate. Dip each veal piece into the breadcrumbs. Turn to coat both sides, patting gently to remove excess crumbs. Place on a separate plate. Repeat until all veal is coated.

Heat 2 tablespoons olive oil in a large nonstick skillet over medium heat. When oil is hot, place a few breaded pieces in the pan and cook for 3 to 4 minutes, or until the edges turn light beige. Turn the veal and cook for 3 minutes more, or until thoroughly cooked. Remove to a serving plate. Repeat with remaining olive oil and veal. Serve warm with lemon wedges.

{ **VARIATIONS** Substitute lamb chops for the veal. }

Salmon with Pesto

PREP TIME: 5 MINUTES   **COOK TIME:** 15 MINUTES   **SERVES:** 4

Rima ate this dish many years ago, the first time she was invited to have dinner at Claudia's. It has been one of her favorites ever since.

1½ pounds salmon fillet

¼ cup pesto, pg 120

1 tablespoon olive oil

Preheat oven to 350°F.

Pour the olive oil in a baking dish. Place salmon in the dish and spread evenly with pesto.

Bake for 15 minutes.

Chicken Madeira

PREP TIME: 10 MINUTES   **COOK TIME:** 10 MINUTES   **SERVES:** 4

This is Claudia's adaptation of her mother's Chicken Saratoga – a recipe so secret that it is only written in the family will.

1 pound boneless, skinless chicken breasts fillets, pg 253

¼ cup all-purpose flour

2 tablespoons butter

½ teaspoon sea salt

Dash freshly ground pepper

¼ cup chicken broth

¼ cup Madeira wine

2 tablespoons balsamic vinegar

1 tablespoon worcestershire sauce

DID YOU KNOW?

Madeira wine is named after a Portuguese Azore island where it is made.

HELPING HANDS

Young children can help measure the chicken broth.

Place the flour on a large plate. Coat each chicken piece with flour and pat gently to remove the excess. Place on a separate plate. Repeat until all chicken is coated.

Melt butter in a large sauté pan over medium heat. When butter begins to foam, place the chicken in the pan and cook for 2 to 3 minutes. Turn chicken and cook for 2 to 3 minutes more or until it is thoroughly cooked. Sprinkle with salt and pepper. Remove to a plate.

Combine remaining sauce ingredients. Add to pan and let simmer over medium heat until reduced by half. Return chicken to pan and turn to coat. Remove from heat and serve.

Glazed Pork Tenderloin

PREP TIME: 10 MINUTES **MARINATE:** 2 HOURS **COOK TIME:** 15 MINUTES **SERVES:** 4 TO 6

When you don't know what to make for dinner, try a pork tenderloin. It is easy to make and tastes good. Roasted or grilled, it can be sliced into medallions or brought to the table for carving.

1 pork tenderloin, about 1 pound

1 tablespoon Marsala wine

1 tablespoon balsamic vinegar

1 tablespoon honey

½ teaspoon sea salt

¼ teaspoon freshly ground pepper

1 small sprig rosemary

1 garlic clove, peeled and minced

2 tablespoons olive oil

Combine Marsala wine, balsamic vinegar, honey, salt, pepper, rosemary and garlic in a small bowl.

Cut away any excess fat or silverskin from the tenderloin. Place in a resealable plastic bag, cover with the wine marinade, and refrigerate for 2 hours.

Take the tenderloin out of the refrigerator 30 minutes before cooking.

Preheat the oven to 425°F.

Heat olive oil in a 12-inch oven-proof skillet over medium heat. Add tenderloin and sear on all sides until well browned, about 5 minutes total.

Coat with remaining marinade and transfer the skillet to the oven. Cook for 15 minutes or until internal temperature measures 150°F.

Transfer the roast to a cutting board, tent with aluminum foil, and let rest for 10 minutes.

Slice into ½-inch thick medallions and serve.

Fondue Chinoise

PREP TIME: 15 MINUTES   **COOK TIME:** SECONDS   **SERVES:** 6

The most fun family meal you will ever have!

2 to 3 pounds eye of round beef, sliced paper thin

6 cups beef broth

3 cups mayonnaise, divided

1 garlic clove, peeled and crushed

1 teaspoon curry powder

1 tablespoon ketchup

1 cup Béarnaise sauce

1 can Sterno (canned cooking fuel)

French Fries, pg 190

PREPARE THE SAUCES:

Mix one cup of mayonnaise with the garlic.
Mix one cup of mayonnaise with the curry powder.
Mix one cup of mayonnaise with the ketchup.

Spoon the sauces and Béarnaise into little ramekins and place on the table.

Pour the beef broth into a saucepan and bring to a boil over medium heat.

Arrange the raw meat on serving platters.

Light the Sterno can under the fondue pot or plug it in. Pour the boiling broth into the fondue pot and place it on the table. Put a teaspoon of your favorite sauce on your plate. Pick up a slice of meat with the fondue fork, roll it around the fork and place it in the hot broth for a few seconds, or until the meat is no longer pink. Remove the fork, put the meat on your plate, dip it in the sauce and enjoy with French Fries and a salad.

DID YOU KNOW?

Traditional Chinese fondue is divided in two phases. The first part is the "fondue," when you cook the meat. The second part is when you cook thin rice noodles and sliced mushrooms in the broth.

HELPING HANDS

Children can help prepare the sauces.

KITCHEN TIP:

Ask your butcher to freeze an eye of round roast for a couple of hours then slice it paper thin.

Scallops with Marsala

PREP TIME: 10 MINUTES **COOK TIME:** 20 MINUTES **SERVES:** 6

When eating tender and delicate scallops, we often forget the beautiful and distinctive shell that protected this mollusk when it lived at sea. Famous painters like Botticelli and Titian captured its intricacies with color and ink, while cooks highlight its flavor with wines and sauces.

1 pound large scallops, rinsed and patted dry

2 tablespoons olive oil

1 garlic clove, peeled and minced

2 small sweet onions, peeled and chopped fine

2 carrots, peeled and chopped fine

2 celery ribs, rinsed and chopped fine

¼ cup chicken broth

1 cup Marsala wine

½ teaspoon sea salt

Dash freshly ground pepper

DID YOU KNOW?

Marsala wine provides a sweet flavor and produces a rich demi-glaze sauce. It is a fortified wine from the Marsala area in Sicily.

HELPING HANDS

Young children can wash the vegetables, older ones can peel and chop them with supervision.

CURIOSITY:

Scallops are a very good source of omega-3 fatty acids which benefit cardiovascular health.

Heat olive oil in a large skillet over low to medium heat. Add garlic, onion, carrot and celery. Sauté in olive oil until vegetables are soft about 5 to 8 minutes. Add broth and simmer for 2 more minutes. Remove to a separate plate, keep warm.

Add scallops and ½ cup Marsala to skillet. Increase heat to medium-high so wine boils. Cook for 4 minutes, allowing liquid to reduce. Turn scallops over and add remaining Marsala. Bring to a boil and reduce one more time, about 4 minutes longer. Serve with sautéed vegetables and couscous, rice or buttered pasta.

Ossobuco

PREP TIME: 20 MINUTES **COOK TIME:** 2 TO 3 HOURS **SERVES:** 4

Also known as braised veal shanks, this delicious dish is characterized by the bone that sits in the middle of the veal shank.

4 veal shanks, about 2 pounds

½ teaspoon sea salt

¼ teaspoon freshly ground pepper

¼ cup all-purpose flour

2 tablespoons butter

¼ cup olive oil

½ onion, peeled and finely chopped, about ½ cup

I carrot, peeled and finely chopped

I celery rib, rinsed and finely chopped

I cup dry white wine OR ½ cup dry sherry and ½ cup Marsala wine

¼ cup plain tomato sauce

2 cups beef broth

FOR THE GREMOLATA:

2 garlic cloves, peeled and minced

2 tablespoons flat-leaf parsley, minced

Zest of one lemon

Salt and pepper the veal on both sides. Place the flour on a small plate, dip each veal shank into the flour, pat gently to remove any excess flour.

Melt butter and olive oil in a large sauté pan over low to medium heat.

Add veal shanks. Sear on all sides, 8 minutes, then remove to a plate and set aside.

Add the onion, carrot and celery to the same pan and sauté over medium heat, stirring often, sauté for 10 minutes until the vegetables are tender.

Return the veal shanks to the pan along with any juices. Add the wine. Cook for 2 minutes, stirring occasionally. Add the tomato sauce and beef broth. Bring to a boil.

Reduce heat to low, cover and simmer for 2 to 3 hours, stirring every 20 to 30 minutes. The meat is cooked when it is very tender and falls away from the bone.

Make the gremolata by mixing the minced garlic, parsley and lemon zest in a small bowl. During the last 10 minutes of cooking, stir it into the Ossobuco. Serve warm, over rice or polenta, with a generous serving of sauce.

Lemon Chicken Piccata

PREP TIME: 5 MINUTES   **COOK TIME:** 10 MINUTES   **SERVES:** 4

This is the perfect dish for a quick dinner. Even though Piccata is often made with veal, we usually make it with chicken because we always have it on hand.

1 pound boneless, skinless chicken breasts fillets, pg 253

½ cup all-purpose flour

4 tablespoons butter

½ teaspoon sea salt

⅛ teaspoon freshly ground pepper

1 tablespoon capers

Juice of one large lemon

¼ cup dry white wine

DID YOU KNOW?

"Piccata" means tart or zesty in Italian.

HELPING HANDS

Young children can help squeeze the lemon juice. Older ones can make the dish with supervision.

Place the flour on a large plate. Place each chicken piece in the flour and pat gently to remove the excess. Place on a separate plate. Repeat until all chicken is coated.

Melt butter in a large nonstick skillet over medium heat. When butter begins to foam, place the chicken in the pan and cook for 2 to 3 minutes. Turn chicken and cook for 2 to 3 minutes more or until it is thoroughly cooked. Sprinkle with salt and pepper.

Add capers and lemon juice. Allow the liquid to evaporate. Stir. Add white wine. Stir to evenly coat chicken. Turn off heat. Cover and let sit 5 minutes so the chicken can absorb the lemon and wine flavors. Serve with cooking sauce.

{ **VARIATIONS** For a traditional dish, substitute 1 pound veal scallopine for the chicken. }

Veal with Sherry

PREP TIME: 10 MINUTES   **COOK TIME:** 30 MINUTES   **SERVES:** 4

Many years ago, Rima made this dish for her friend, Michelle, and she loved it. She asked for the recipe and it became one of her "go-to" family favorites. When it was time to write the cookbook, we had a question so we called Michelle and asked for "her" Veal with Sherry recipe.

KITCHEN TIP:

This dish is a good one to make ahead. Prepare the recipe and stop before adding the cream. Put the sauce and the veal in the refrigerator. Before serving, heat the sauce, add the cream and continue.

HELPING HANDS

Young children can flour the veal. Older ones can slice the mushrooms.

1 pound veal scaloppine, about 6 pieces

½ cup all-purpose flour

2 tablespoons olive oil

2 tablespoons butter

½ teaspoon sea salt

½ onion, peeled and diced, about ½ cup

1 8-ounce package white mushrooms, sliced

¾ cup dry sherry

½ cup heavy whipping cream

Place the flour on a large plate. Place each veal piece in the flour and pat gently to remove the excess. Place on a separate plate. Repeat until all veal is coated.

Heat olive oil and butter in a large skillet over medium heat. Cook the veal for 2 to 3 minutes on one side, then 1 to 2 minutes on the other side. Sprinkle with salt. Remove to a warm platter.

To the same pan, add onion and cook for 5 minutes, stirring occasionally. Add mushrooms and cook for 5 more minutes, stirring occasionally. Add Sherry, scraping pan to incorporate all the browned bits. Let simmer until the liquid has reduced by half — about 6 to 7 minutes.

Reduce heat to low, add cream, bring to a gentle boil, then add the veal. Cover and let cook for 5 minutes. Serve warm with white rice and a vegetable.

VARIATIONS If you prefer, you can substitute boneless, skinless chicken breasts for the veal.

Chicken Pinwheels

PREP TIME: 30 MINUTES   **COOK TIME:** 20 MINUTES   **SERVES:** 4

Stuffing and rolling the chicken before cooking, then slicing it crosswise, gives it a whimsical pinwheel design.

DID YOU KNOW?

"Pinwheels for Peace" was started in 2005 by two teachers in Florida. Every September, students from all over the world "plant" hand-crafted pinwheels on International Peace Day.

HELPING HANDS

Children should always wash their hands with soap and water after handling raw chicken.

KITCHEN TIP:

You can bake the chicken rolls in an oven pre-heated to 350°F for about 25 minutes, instead of cooking them on the stove.

FOR THE FILLING:

4 ounces frozen spinach, defrosted, about ½ cup

2 tablespoons olive oil

1 garlic clove, peeled and minced

⅛ teaspoon sea salt

Dash freshly ground pepper

1 tablespoon cream cheese

2 tablespoons grated Parmesan cheese

FOR THE CHICKEN:

1½ pounds boneless skinless chicken breasts, pg 253

2 tablespoons butter

½ teaspoon sea salt

⅛ teaspoon freshly ground pepper

6 to 8 wooden toothpicks

2 tablespoons Marsala wine

2 tablespoons chicken broth

PREPARE THE SPINACH FILLING:

Squeeze the spinach with your hands to remove any excess water.

Heat 2 tablespoons olive oil in a medium nonstick skillet. Add garlic and drained spinach and cook for 3 minutes over low to medium heat. Season with salt and pepper. Remove from heat. Transfer to a bowl and stir in cream cheese and Parmesan cheese. Set aside.

PREPARE THE CHICKEN:

Butterfly the chicken, page 250. Sprinkle chicken with the sea salt and pepper.

Spread 2 tablespoons of spinach filling over surface of each breast without getting to close to the edge. Beginning at the short end, roll each piece of chicken "jellyroll" fashion. Secure with a wooden toothpick.

{ **VARIATIONS** Stir in some dried cherries or chopped sun-dried tomatoes into the spinach filling. }

Melt butter in a large skillet, over low to medium heat. Add chicken rolls, seam part down, and cook for 10 minutes, turning once.

Add Marsala wine and chicken broth. Cover and cook for 10 more minutes, turning each chicken roll halfway through.

Remove chicken rolls to a cutting board. Let cool for a few minutes.

Remove toothpicks. Cut into ½-inch thick slices and transfer to a serving platter. Serve with sauce from pan.

Sea Bass in Parchment

PREP TIME: 10 MINUTES   **COOK TIME:** 20 TO 25 MINUTES   **SERVES:** 4

In Italy, this cooking technique is called Cartoccio all'Isolana. In Europe, fish are smaller so we cook them whole. This is a fillet version of this very popular Italian dish.

DID YOU KNOW?

Sea bass are the largest family of fish in the world.

HELPING HANDS

Children can help mix the oil, lemon and herbs.

CURIOSITY:

Chilean sea bass is not a member of the sea bass family.

1½ pounds sea bass

1 large piece of parchment paper, about 15 x 30-inches

1 zucchini squash, rinsed and sliced very thin

1 potato, peeled and sliced very thin

1 tomato, rinsed and sliced very thin

½ cup olive oil

Juice of one lemon

1 teaspoon sea salt

Freshly ground pepper

4 small sprigs fresh oregano, chopped

4 small sprigs fresh thyme, chopped

Preheat oven to 400°F.

Place sliced vegetables on the center of the parchment paper. Mix oil, lemon, salt, pepper and herbs in a small bowl. Sprinkle half the oil mixture over the vegetables, tossing until well-coated. Place the sea bass on the vegetables. Sprinkle with remaining oil mixture.

Fold the paper to make a sealed package. Bake 20 to 25 minutes. Cut parchment with a sharp knife and serve immediately.

Leg of Lamb

PREP TIME: 10 MINUTES **COOK TIME:** 2 TO 3 HOURS **REST TIME:** 15 MINUTES **SERVES:** 8 TO 10

Available year round, lamb makes a perfect choice for every season and occasion. In Italy, it is often eaten at Easter.

1 leg of lamb , 6 to 8 pounds

4 small sprigs fresh rosemary

10 garlic cloves, peeled

½ cup olive oil, divided

1 tablespoon sea salt

½ teaspoon freshly ground pepper

Preheat oven to 500°F.

Trim most of the fat from the leg of lamb.

Remove the leaves from the rosemary sprigs. Place in a blender, or chop finely by hand. Add garlic gloves and ¼ cup olive oil. Blend.

Generously salt and pepper lamb on all sides.

Pour remaining olive oil into a roasting pan. Add the roast, fat side down. With your hands, spread the garlic mixture all over the lamb.

Cook for 15 minutes then reduce heat to 400°F and continue cooking for 2½ hours or until internal temperature measures 155°F for medium-well.

Remove from oven, tent with aluminum foil and let rest for 15 minutes before serving.

Grilled Chicken with Herbs

PREP TIME: 5 MINUTES   **COOK TIME:** 15 MINUTES   **SERVES:** 4

This recipe was given to us by our New York friend and great chef, Francine. It's simple, healthy and quick to make.

I pound boneless, skinless chicken breasts fillets, pg 253

I tablespoon dried oregano

I tablespoon dried thyme

½ teaspoon sea salt

Dash freshly ground pepper

½ cup extra-virgin olive oil

Juice of one lemon

KITCHEN TIP:

Make sure the herbs are ground very fine.

HELPING HANDS

Children can help press the herbs on the chicken. Make sure they wash their hands well after doing so.

Turn on the grill to medium heat.

Place chicken on a plate. Rub herbs between your palms until finely ground. Coat each chicken fillet with the herbs, pressing firmly with your hands. Season with salt and pepper.

Grill chicken for 3 to 4 minutes on each side, or until thoroughly cooked. Remove the chicken to a serving plate. Mix extra-virgin olive oil and lemon juice in a small bowl. Pour over chicken. Tent with aluminum foil. Let rest 5 minutes before serving.

{ **VARIATIONS** This dish works well if you substitute salmon fillet for chicken. }

Tagliata

PREP TIME: 30 MINUTES   **COOK TIME:** 30 MINUTES   **REST TIME:** 10 MINUTES   **SERVES:** 4 TO 6

Referred to as Tagliata di Manzo, this mouth-watering version of a grilled porterhouse steak originated in Florence. Typically it is served with cannellini beans, but nowadays it is often served with arugula salad.

DID YOU KNOW?

The dish got its name from the Italian "tagliata" which means to cut, because before you serve it, you cut it into thin slices.

2 large porterhouse steaks, thick cut – about 2 inches

3 tablespoons olive oil

3 small sprigs fresh rosemary

Sea salt

Freshly ground pepper

KITCHEN TIP:

Slice meat on a cutting board with a liquid moat to collect the juices as you slice the meat.

Rub fresh ground pepper and sea salt on the meat, then with a sprig of rosemary brush it with olive oil. Let sit for at least ½ hour with the rosemary under and over it.

Prepare a hot barbeque. Grill the steak on one side until seared, about 5 minutes. Turn over and sear the other side for 5 minutes. Reduce the temperature of the grill and continue grilling for another 15 to 20 minutes or until internal temperature measures 145°F for medium-rare. Remove steaks from grill, place on a cutting board and tent with aluminum foil. Let rest for 10 minutes. Slice into ½-inch thick pieces and serve.

NOTE: Tagliata is best enjoyed medium rare.

Grilled Tri-tip

PREP TIME: 5 MINUTES   **COOK TIME:** 30 TO 40 MINUTES   **SERVES:** 4 TO 5

What could be easier than turning on the grill? When you start with a flavorful cut of meat, a simple cooking approach works best.

1 tri-tip roast, about 2 pounds

Sea salt

Freshly ground pepper

Prepare a hot grill.

Generously sprinkle the tri-tip roast with salt and pepper on all sides. Place meat on the hot grill and cook 15 to 20 minutes per side. Adjust the flame, or raise the grill so the meat does not burn.

When internal temperature measures 145°F for medium-rare, remove tri-tip from grill, place on a cutting board with a liquid moat and tent with aluminum foil. Let rest for 10 minutes before slicing across the grain.

Sole Meunier

PREP TIME: 5 MINUTES   **COOK TIME:** 15 MINUTES   **SERVES:** 4

Sole is a type of food that tastes best with a simple preparation. This dish features flaky white flesh sizzled in butter with a delicate coating of lemon sauce.

1 pound sole fillets

2 tablespoons butter

½ cup all-purpose flour

¼ teaspoon sea salt

Dash freshly ground pepper

FOR THE BUTTER SAUCE:

2 tablespoons butter

2 sprigs flat-leaf parsley, rinsed and chopped fine

Juice of ½ lemon

KITCHEN TIP:
You can use whole sole since it is fairly easy to remove the bones after it is cooked.

HELPING HANDS
Young children can coat the sole with flour, older ones can prepare this dish with supervision.

Place the flour on a large plate. Coat sole fillets with flour and pat gently to remove the excess. Place on a separate plate.

Melt 2 tablespoons butter in a large nonstick skillet over medium heat. When butter begins to foam, place the fish in the pan and cook for 1 minute. Reduce heat and continue cooking for 5 minutes. Turn the sole over and repeat the same procedure. Season with salt and pepper.

Meanwhile, make the butter sauce. Melt 2 tablespoons butter in a small nonstick skillet over low to medium heat. When butter begins to foam, add parsley. Cook for one minute. Do not let the butter burn. Remove from heat, wait for one minute, then stir in the lemon juice. Pour over cooked sole and serve.

Chicken Roman Style

PREP TIME: 5 MINUTES   **COOK TIME:** 45 MINUTES   **SERVES:** 4

We served this dish at the family-style dinner we hosted for the Nobel Peace Laureates at Rima's house in Rome because we wanted everyone to feel "at home." It worked! It will be our favorite "feel at home" dish forever.

1½ pounds boneless, skinless chicken thighs

2 tablespoons olive oil

4 garlic cloves, peeled and minced

1 tablespoon capers

1 teaspoon dried oregano

1 teaspoon sea salt

Dash freshly ground pepper

1 cup dry white wine

1 15-ounce can, good quality tomato sauce

Rinse chicken pieces and dry with paper towel. Set aside.

Heat olive oil in a large stock pot over medium heat. Add chicken and cook gently for 5 minutes. Reduce heat. Add garlic, capers, oregano, salt, pepper and mix. Let the chicken soak up all the flavors, about 10 minutes. Add wine and let evaporate.

Add tomato sauce, ¼ cup of water and cover. Cook for 20 to 25 minutes stirring occasionally until the tomato sauce has concentrated and the chicken is thoroughly cooked.

Roast Chicken with Vegetables

PREP TIME: 20 MINUTES   **COOK TIME:** 1 TO 2 HOURS   **REST TIME:** 15 MINUTES   **SERVES:** 4 TO 6

Nothing says "time for dinner" like the inviting aroma of a chicken roasting in the oven.

1 roasting chicken, 5 pounds, completely defrosted

1 onion, peeled and cut into eighths

2 carrots, peeled and cut on the diagonal into 1-inch chunks

2 ribs celery, rinsed and cut on the diagonal into 1-inch chunks

4 red potatoes, rinsed and cut into quarters

½ small butternut squash, peeled, seeded and cut into 1-inch chunks

8 garlic cloves, divided

4 small sprigs fresh rosemary, divided

4 small sprigs fresh thyme, divided

4 fresh sage leaves, divided

4 tablespoons olive oil, divided

2 teaspoons sea salt, divided

Freshly ground pepper

CURIOSITY:
When first cultivated, carrots were red, yellow and even purple. Look for them at your local market, they taste great!

HELPING HANDS
Young children can help stir the vegetables. Older ones can peel and cut them with supervision.

DID YOU KNOW?
Roasting a chicken with vegetables is an easy way to make a complete meal!

Preheat oven to 450°F.

Place onion, carrots, celery, potatoes, butternut squash, 4 garlic cloves, 2 sprigs each of rosemary and thyme and 2 sage leaves in a large roasting pan or baking dish. Drizzle with 2 tablespoons olive oil, 1 teaspoon salt and pepper. Stir to coat well, then move vegetables to the side to make room for the chicken.

Remove giblets, neck and tail fat from the chicken. Rinse chicken under cold running water. Drain and pat dry with paper towel. Place 4 garlic cloves, 2 sprigs each of rosemary and thyme and 2 sage leaves inside the cavity of the chicken. Place it in the center of the pan, breast side up, and drizzle with remaining 2 tablespoons of olive oil. Season chicken with remaining salt and more pepper. Place pan in the middle of the oven and roast for 30 minutes.

Reduce heat to 375°F and continue cooking for 50 to 75 minutes or until the internal temperature of the thigh measures 180°F.

Tent with aluminum foil. Let rest for 15 minutes before serving with cooked vegetables.

NOTE: Pour pan juices into a fat separator or degreasing cup so the fat floats to the top. Strain the juices into a small saucepan and simmer over medium heat for 2 to 3 minutes until reduced by half. Pour this concentrated sauce over the chicken just before serving.

vegetables

WE KNOW it is at the table that we teach good manners. By encouraging children to try new foods, we inspire them to explore. By serving simple foods on fancy plates, we show them how any meal can become an elaborate feast.

Carrots by Rose

PREP TIME: 5 MINUTES **COOK TIME:** 25 MINUTES **SERVES:** 4 TO 6

Cooked carrots have never tasted better! Rose, Claudia's mother is famous for making exceptional food. When it comes to cooking, she has the "Midas Touch!"

8 medium carrots, peeled and sliced into ⅛-inch rounds

2 tablespoons butter

¼ onion, peeled and chopped fine, about ¼ cup

¼ cup dry white wine

¼ teaspoon sea salt

½ cup freshly grated Parmesan cheese

Place 1 cup of water in a medium saucepan and bring to a boil over high heat. Add sliced carrots, reduce heat to low, cover and simmer for 5 minutes.

Meanwhile, melt butter in a medium, nonstick skillet over low heat. Add onion. Cook for 5 minutes, stirring occasionally.

Drain carrots and add to onions. Add wine and stir. When liquid has evaporated, add salt. Continue cooking, stirring occasionally for about 20 minutes. Remove from heat and sprinkle with Parmesan cheese. Stir to melt.

DID YOU KNOW?

Carrots are an excellent source of beta-carotene. They are also a good source of fiber.

HELPING HANDS

Young children can help rinse the carrots, older ones can peel them.

KITCHEN TIP:

You can substitute chicken broth for the white wine.

Brussels Sprouts

PREP TIME: 15 MINUTES **COOK TIME:** 90 MINUTES **SERVES:** 4 TO 6

Rima was pleasantly surprised to discover a delicious way to cook Brussels sprouts after her friend Micki prepared them for her. This recipe is now shared and enjoyed by many of her friends.

DID YOU KNOW?

Phytonutrients found in Brussels sprouts enhance the activity of the body's natural defense systems to protect against disease.

HELPING HANDS

Young children can help mix the sprouts and the olive oil with their hands.

KITCHEN TIP:

Brussel sprouts taste best when fresh while they are still on the stalk.

1 pound fresh Brussels sprouts, rinsed

¼ cup olive oil

¼ teaspoon sea salt

Dash freshly ground pepper

2 tablespoons breadcrumbs

Preheat oven to 400°F.

Cut the ends off the sprouts, then in half lengthwise.

Place them in a baking sheet with a one inch rim. Sprinkle with olive oil, salt and pepper. Mix well. Bake for 1½ hours. Top with bread crumbs and bake for another 10 minutes.

Potatoes Gratin

PREP TIME: 20 MINUTES **COOK TIME:** 90 MINUTES **SERVES:** 6 TO 8

This recipe originated in France, but it is so good that it is now loved internationally. There are many versions of potatoes gratin, but we find this the easiest and tastiest.

2 pounds baking potatoes, peeled, sliced thin, rinsed and drained

2 tablespoons butter

I batch Béchamel White Sauce, pg 97

½ cup heavy whipping cream, divided

I teaspoon sea salt

Freshly ground pepper

½ cup grated Parmesan cheese

Preheat oven to 350°F.

Butter the bottom of a 9 x 13-inch baking pan. Make a layer with half of the potatoes. Sprinkle with salt and pepper. Top with half the Béchamel White Sauce and ¼ cup the cream.

Repeat to make a second layer. Sprinkle with Parmesan cheese.

Bake for 1½ hours or until the potatoes are soft. Let rest 5 minutes.

DID YOU KNOW?

Boiled potatoes may be an effective treatment for skin wounds. These benefits are especially helpful in some third-world countries where modern skin graft procedures are not available.

HELPING HANDS

Older children can peel the potatoes.

KITCHEN TIP:

The best way to cut these potatoes is using a mandoline. See glossary page 252.

Baked Vegetables

PREP TIME: 10 MINUTES **COOK TIME:** 30 MINUTES **SERVES:** 4 TO 6

For many years, Claudia made this delicious and incredibly easy recipe with tomatoes. Then we realized it would taste great with other vegetables. Try it when you want to impress your family!

2 large tomatoes, rinsed and cut in half

1 small zucchini squash, rinsed and cut in half lengthwise

1 small summer squash, rinsed and cut in half lengthwise

1 small eggplant, rinsed and cut in half lengthwise

1 bell pepper, rinsed and cut into 6 wedges

¼ cup dry white wine

½ teaspoon sea salt

Dash freshly ground pepper

½ cup breadcrumbs

½ cup grated Parmesan cheese

2 tablespoons flat-leaf parsley, chopped fine

½ cup extra-virgin olive oil, divided

4 ounces mozzarella or fontina cheese, sliced into 16 thin pieces

¼ cup pine nuts, optional

Preheat oven to 325°F. Lightly grease a 9 x 13-inch glass baking pan.

Place vegetables in the pan. Drizzle evenly with white wine then sprinkle with salt and pepper.

Mix breadcrumbs, Parmesan cheese, parsley and ¼ cup olive oil in a medium bowl. Spoon about 2 tablespoons of bread crumb mixture onto each vegetable, using a spoon or your fingers to pat it down. Drizzle with remaining olive oil.

Bake for 20 minutes, top each vegetable with a slice of cheese and pine nuts. Bake for 10 more minutes.

Sautéed Peas

PREP TIME: 5 MINUTES   **COOK TIME:** 10 MINUTES   **SERVES:** 4 TO 6

This is one of the simplest and most delicious recipes you can make with your family. We always keep peas in the freezer so that in 10 minutes we have a healthy side dish.

1 tablespoon butter

1 tablespoon olive oil

½ onion, peeled and chopped fine, about ½ cup

1 pound frozen peas

¼ teaspoon sea salt

Dash freshly ground pepper

Melt butter and olive oil in a large, heavy-bottomed skillet, over medium heat. Add the onions and sauté for 5 minutes. Add the peas. Sprinkle with salt and pepper, cover and cook for 5 to 8 minutes, stirring occasionally.

Creamed Spinach

PREP TIME: 10 MINUTES   **COOK TIME:** 20 MINUTES   **SERVES:** 4

Creamed spinach is nutritious and complements many entrées. Children who are not fans of plain spinach will love this creation.

3 pounds fresh spinach, rinsed OR one 16-ounce package frozen chopped spinach

2 tablespoons butter

½ onion, peeled and chopped fine, about ½ cup

¼ teaspoon sea salt

Dash freshly ground pepper

Dash ground nutmeg

2 tablespoons flour

1 cup milk

For fresh spinach: put it in a large pot, with 2 cups of boiling water. Cover and cook over high heat for 4 to 5 minutes, stirring often. Remove from heat, drain and let cool. Squeeze out any excess water.

For frozen spinach: defrost and drain. Squeeze out any excess water.

Melt butter in a large nonstick skillet, over low to medium heat. Add onion and sauté until translucent, about 5 minutes. Add drained spinach and sauté for 5 more minutes, stirring occasionally. Add salt, pepper and nutmeg. Sprinkle the flour over the spinach and stir it in well. Slowly add the milk and stir until well blended. Cook until the mixture is creamy, about 5 more minutes, stirring occasionally. Taste and adjust seasonings. Serve warm.

DID YOU KNOW?

There actually is no cream in the recipe. Cooking the milk with the flour and butter gives a creamy consistency.

HELPING HANDS

Children can help clean the fresh spinach leaves.

CURIOSITY:

Spinach's secret weapon, lutein is proven effective in promoting healthy eyesight.

VARIATIONS Stir in ¼ cup of grated cheddar cheese and/or ¼ cup cooked, crumbled bacon or pancetta before serving.

Roasted Asparagus

PREP TIME: 5 MINUTES **COOK TIME:** 10 MINUTES **SERVES:** 4

The easiest recipe ever! It became a favorite after our friend David shared it with us.

KITCHEN TIP:

Snap off the last 2 inches of each asparagus spear so you serve the most tender part.

HELPING HANDS

Children can help drizzle the olive oil.

1 pound asparagus, medium thickness, rinsed

¼ cup olive oil

½ tablespoon garlic salt

Freshly ground pepper

Preheat oven to 400°F.

Arrange the asparagus spears in one layer on a baking sheet. Drizzle with olive oil. Sprinkle evenly with garlic salt and pepper.

Bake for 4 minutes, turn over each one and bake for 5 more minutes.

DID YOU KNOW?

You can refresh asparagus spears by soaking them in cold water.

{ **VARIATIONS** Before serving sprinkle with ½ cup blue cheese crumbles. }

Roasted Potatoes

PREP TIME: 10 MINUTES   **COOK TIME:** 60 MINUTES   **SERVES:** 6

Our good friend, Marianne, makes the best roasted potatoes ever! We asked her for her secret recipe and she was so kind to share it with us. Make sure that each piece of potato is completely coated with oil and sits away from its neighbor on the baking sheet.

2 pounds new or red potatoes, rinsed and cut into 2-inch pieces

1 cup olive oil or enough to coat each potato

2 tablespoons balsamic vinegar

3 garlic cloves, peeled and grated

2 sprigs fresh rosemary, chopped *very* fine

1 tablespoon sea salt

1 teaspoon freshly ground pepper

Preheat oven to 400°F.

Mix together oil, vinegar, garlic, rosemary, salt and pepper in a medium bowl.

Place the potatoes in a large baking pan. Pour the oil mixture on them and mix them with your hands until each potato piece is completely coated. Spread in one layer so they are not touching each other.

Bake for 1 hour, stirring every 15 minutes or until cooked.

DID YOU KNOW?
Potatoes contain glutathione, an antioxidant that may help protect against cancer.

HELPING HANDS
Young children can help mix the oil and the potatoes with their hands. Older ones can prepare the marinade.

CURIOSITY:
The potato plant produces more nutritious food in harsher climates than any other major crop.

Caramelized Cauliflower

PREP TIME: 10 MINUTES **COOK TIME:** 30 MINUTES **SERVES:** 6

Claudia first tasted this dish when her friend, Joan, made it for a party that they were both catering. The simple yet sublime flavors guarantee that it will remain a party favorite.

I head cauliflower, rinsed and cut into about 10 florets

2 tablespoons butter, melted

¼ cup blue cheese crumbles

¼ cup grated Parmesan cheese

Heat 2 cups water in a medium saucepan over high heat. When boiling, add cauliflower florets and cover. Steam for 5 minutes. Remove from heat and drain.

Preheat oven to 325°F.

Place steamed cauliflower in a single layer in an oven-proof 9 x 9-inch baking dish, stem side down. Cover evenly with melted butter and cheeses.

Bake for 20 to 30 minutes, or until light brown. Serve warm.

DID YOU KNOW?

Cauliflower is high in vitamin C and is a good source of folic acid. It pairs well with Béchamel sauce, breadcrumbs, curry, garlic, olive oil or parsley.

HELPING HANDS

Older children can rinse and cut the cauliflower.

Broccoli

PREP TIME: 5 MINUTES **COOK TIME:** 5 MINUTES **SERVES:** 4

I head broccoli, rinsed and stems cut off, about 3 cups florets

2 tablespoons extra-virgin olive oil

Sea salt to taste

Put 1 cup of water in a medium saucepan and place on the stove over high heat. When the water boils, add broccoli and cover. Steam for 3 minutes. Drain. Drizzle with olive oil and season with salt. Serve immediately.

HELPING HANDS

Children can help rinse the broccoli. Older ones can cut it with supervision.

DID YOU KNOW?

Broccoli is an excellent source of vitamins A and C, as well as riboflavin, calcium and iron.

{ **VARIATIONS** Before serving, sprinkle with lemon juice, lemon zest or grated cheese. }

Peperonata

PREP TIME: 10 MINUTES   **COOK TIME:** 90 MINUTES   **SERVES:** 4 TO 6

This original peasant dish goes well with meats, polenta or as a bruschetta topping.
This colorful dish can be served hot or at room temperature.

½ cup olive oil

1 onion, peeled, sliced in ½-inch half-moon slices

2 garlic cloves, peeled

3 large bell peppers, cored and sliced into ½-inch strips

¼ teaspoon sea salt

Dash freshly ground pepper

1 15-ounce can diced tomatoes

Heat olive oil in a large nonstick skillet over low to medium heat. Add onion and garlic and sauté for 2 to 3 minutes. Take out the garlic, then add the peppers and sauté for 10 to 15 minutes. Season with salt and pepper. Add diced tomatoes, cover, reduce heat to low and cook for 1½ hours, stirring occasionally. Taste and adjust for salt and pepper. Enjoy warm or at room temperature.

Mashed Potatoes

PREP TIME: 15 MINUTES   **COOK TIME:** 40 MINUTES   **SERVES:** 6

Anthony, Rima's husband, is definitely the best mashed potato maker ever. Nobody even tries to make them when he is around. His best "unkept" secret is adding tons of butter and cream!

3 pounds russet potatoes, peeled and cut in 2 inch pieces

½ cup butter, 1 stick

2 cups milk or heavy whipping cream

Sea salt

Freshly ground pepper

Place the potatoes in a large pot with plenty of water to cover. Bring to a boil over high heat. Cook for 25 to 30 minutes or until soft.

Drain. Put them back in the same pot and "mash" with a hand-held mixer or potato masher. For the fluffiest potatoes, be sure they are thoroughly mashed before adding any other ingredient.

Add the butter, half the milk and some salt and pepper. Keep mixing while adding the rest of the milk. Taste and adjust for salt and pepper.

Serve immediately!

CURIOSITY:

The more intense the yellow color of the flesh, the higher the vitamin A level, which promotes good vision, healthy skin and an improved immune system.

HELPING HANDS

Children can help mash the potatoes.

KITCHEN TIP:

Peel away any green flesh from the potato. It indicates a concentration of solanine which can be toxic at high levels.

desserts

WE KNOW great meals begin in the kitchen, are enjoyed at the family table and connect the family forever. We must return to this family center for the well-being of our children, our community and our world.

Fruit Salad

PREP TIME: 20 MINUTES **SERVES:** 6

Fruit salad makes a great dessert or snack anytime of the year. The orange juice in this recipe acts as a conductor for this symphony of flavors.

1 banana, peeled and sliced

1 pear, peeled, cored and cut into small dice

4 apricots, rinsed and pitted

2 kiwi, peeled and cut into slices

8 strawberries, rinsed and stems removed

¼ cup orange juice

Place the fruit in a large serving bowl. Toss with orange juice.

CURIOSITY:
Apricots were first grown in China more than 4,000 years ago.

HELPING HANDS
Young children can help pick the fruit and pour the orange juice. Older ones can peel and cut the fruit with supervision.

KITCHEN TIP
If making the salad ahead of time, add the banana just before serving.

{ **VARIATIONS** Be creative and substitute with your favorite fruit in season. }

Mocha Marble Cake

PREP TIME: 20 MINUTES   **COOK TIME:** 60 MINUTES   **SERVES:** 16

This cake is a fun dessert to serve. The yummy taste and intriguing pattern of chocolate and vanilla dough swirled together promise quick approval from family and friends.

FOR THE CAKE:

1 cup butter, 2 sticks, room temperature

1 cup sugar

½ cup brown sugar

3 large eggs

1 cup sour cream

1 tablespoon pure vanilla extract

3 cups all-purpose flour

1 teaspoon baking soda

1 teaspoon baking powder

¾ teaspoon sea salt

1 cup semisweet chocolate chips, melted

2 tablespoons strong coffee

OPTIONAL GARNISH:

½ cup semisweet chocolate chips, melted

2 tablespoons powdered sugar

Preheat oven to 350°F. Grease and flour an 8 to 10-cup bundt pan.

Beat butter, sugar and brown sugar in a large bowl with an electric mixer until light and fluffy, about 3 minutes. Add eggs, one at a time, mixing well after each addition. Beat in sour cream and vanilla.

Stir together flour, baking soda, baking powder and salt in a medium bowl. Add to cake in three additions, mixing gently after each addition.

Place 2 cups of batter in a small bowl and stir in melted chocolate and coffee. Alternately, drop the different batters into prepared pan. Run a knife through the cake a few times, swirling the batter just a little.

Bake cake for 50 to 60 minutes, until a tester inserted in the center of the cake comes out clean. Allow cake to cool completely before turning it out.

Garnish with melted chocolate or powdered sugar.

Chocolate Chip Cookies

PREP TIME: 15 MINUTES   **COOK TIME:** 12 MINUTES   **MAKES:** 36

This is Claudia's famous recipe for the most irresistible chocolate chip cookies you will ever eat!

1 cup butter, 2 sticks, room temperature

2 cups sugar

2 large eggs

1 tablespoon pure vanilla extract

3 cups all-purpose flour

1 teaspoon cream of tartar

1 teaspoon baking soda

½ teaspoon sea salt

3 cups semisweet chocolate chips

HELPING HANDS

Children can help measure the chocolate chips and make the dough into balls for baking.

DID YOU KNOW?

The cream of tartar reacts with the baking soda to create the perfect soft and round cookie.

KITCHEN TIP

Use real butter! The proportion of butter to flour guarantees a soft texture.

Preheat oven to 350°F. Grease three baking sheets or line with silicone baking mats.

Combine room temperature butter and sugar in a large mixing bowl. Beat with an electric mixer fitted with a paddle attachment until light and fluffy, about 3 minutes. Add eggs one at a time, beating well after each addition. Beat in vanilla.

Stir flour, cream of tartar, baking soda and salt in a separate bowl. Add to butter mixture and beat on low speed until well-mixed, about 30 seconds.

Mix in chocolate chips. Using a large spoon or ice cream scoop, make 36 balls of dough and place evenly on prepared baking sheets. (The rounder the balls, the plumper the cookies.)

Bake for 10 to 12 minutes, rotating once during baking. Remove from oven and let cool on a wire rack. Best if eaten on the same day!

{ **VARIATIONS** For a more nutritious cookie, substitute 1 cup of whole wheat pastry flour and/or 1 cup of oat flour for the same amount of all-purpose flour. }

Harvest Apple Crisp

PREP TIME: 20 MINUTES **COOK TIME:** 50 MINUTES **SERVES:** 8

This yummy apple dessert is easier to make than pie, but just as tasty! Serve warm with a generous scoop of vanilla or caramel ice cream.

6 large apples, rinsed, peeled and sliced thin

¼ cup apple juice

3 tablespoons sugar

1 teaspoon cinnamon

FOR THE TOPPING:

⅓ cup all-purpose flour

⅓ cup whole wheat pastry flour

⅓ cup rolled oats

½ cup brown sugar, packed

1 teaspoon cinnamon

½ teaspoon sea salt

¼ cup butter, ½ stick, cut into fourths

Preheat oven to 350°F. Grease or butter a 9 x 9-inch square baking pan.

Layer sliced apples in the bottom of the pan. Sprinkle with apple juice, sugar and cinnamon.

Stir together flour, whole wheat pastry flour, oats, brown sugar, cinnamon and salt in a medium bowl. Add butter and "cut in" with 2 knives or a pastry blender until it is crumbly and the butter pieces are the size of peas. (Alternatively, use a food processor fitted with a steel blade.)

Spread topping evenly over apples. Bake for 45 to 50 minutes until top is light brown and the apples are tender when pricked with a fork.

Strawberry Tiramisu

PREP TIME: 45 MINUTES   **FRIDGE TIME:** 4 TO 6 HOURS   **SERVES:** 12

This delicious combination of cookies, strawberries and cream is a variation of the original tiramisu, made with coffee and shaved chocolate. Make it a few hours ahead and serve the same day.

6 large eggs

½ cup sugar

16 ounces mascarpone cheese

1 12-ounce package Italian ladyfinger cookies, about 18 cookies

1 cup cold water

2 teaspoons cognac

FOR THE STRAWBERRY COULIS:

1 16-ounce bag frozen strawberries

4 tablespoons sugar

FOR THE GARNISH:

1 pint strawberries, rinsed and sliced

4 tablespoons powdered sugar, optional

DID YOU KNOW?

Strawberries are naturally high in vitamins and minerals, low in calories, naturally sweet and easy to find.

HELPING HANDS

Young children can wash the strawberries, older ones can cut them with supervision.

KITCHEN TIP:

Young children and people in at-risk health groups should avoid eating foods that contain raw or lightly-cooked eggs.

PREPARE THE COULIS:

Place the strawberries with their juice and sugar in a medium saucepan. Stir to combine. Cover and cook over low to medium heat for 45 minutes, stirring occasionally. Remove from heat and allow to cool. Blend until smooth.

PREPARE THE TIRAMISU:

Meanwhile, separate the eggs. Put the egg whites in a large mixing bowl, set aside.

Place the egg yolks in a separate mixing bowl. Add sugar and beat with an electric mixer until pale yellow and fluffy, at least 5 minutes. Add mascarpone and beat until creamy.

With clean beaters, beat the egg whites until very stiff. Using a large rubber spatula, fold them into the mascarpone mixture until they are well incorporated.

Mix water and cognac in a bowl big enough to fit one cookie. Quickly dip one cookie into the water, flip it, then place in a 9 x 13-inch glass baking dish. Repeat until you have one complete layer of cookies. Top with mascarpone mixture. Cover with plastic and refrigerate for 4 to 6 hours.

TO SERVE:

Decorate tiramisu with sliced strawberries and drizzle individual plates with strawberry coulis. Sprinkle with powdered sugar.

Affogato al Caffé

PREP TIME: 5 MINUTES   **SERVES:** 4

We've included this recipe because we believe more people should know about this absolutely delicious ice cream dessert!

CURIOSITY:

In Italian, "Affogato al caffé" means drowned in coffee.

DID YOU KNOW?

Coffee is America's number one source of antioxidants which act like an army protecting you from toxic free radicals.

I pint good quality vanilla ice cream

I cup espresso coffee, cooled a bit

Divide the ice cream among 4 glasses. Top each with ¼ cup espresso coffee. Serve immediately. Simply unbelievable!

Dark Chocolate Cupcakes

PREP TIME: 10 MINUTES   **COOK TIME:** 15 MINUTES   **MAKES:** 12

Serve these rich chocolate cupcakes during the week to make a routine family night seem more special. Their dense and velvety texture will be a hit with chocolate lovers.

½ cup butter, 1 stick

6 ounces bittersweet chocolate, broken into small pieces

2 tablespoons water

2 large eggs

½ cup sugar

1 tablespoon pure vanilla extract

½ cup all-purpose flour

¼ teaspoon baking powder

¼ teaspoon sea salt

2 tablespoons powdered sugar

KITCHEN TIP:

Melt the butter, chocolate, and water in a glass bowl in the microwave on 50% power, for 2 minutes. Stir to mix.

HELPING HANDS

Young children can help count out and place the cupcake liners in the baking pan and help dust with powdered sugar.

Preheat oven to 350°F. Line a 12-count muffin pan with paper liners.

Combine butter, chocolate and water in a small saucepan and place over low heat to melt, stirring constantly. When melted, remove from heat.

Beat eggs, sugar and vanilla in a large bowl with an electric mixer until fluffy, about 3 minutes. Add melted chocolate and mix.

Stir together flour, baking powder and salt in a separate bowl, then add to the egg batter and beat on low speed until just combined. Divide batter evenly among muffin cups.

Bake for 20 minutes or until a knife inserted in the middle comes out clean. Remove from oven and let cool on a wire rack. Dust with powdered sugar.

Nonno's Polenta Cake

PREP TIME: 20 MINUTES **COOK TIME:** 60 MINUTES **SERVES:** 12

Also known as Amor di Polenta, this recipe is named for all grandfathers who appreciate a great dessert and specifically for Claudia's father, Mario, who is from the town of Bergamo, Italy where this recipe originated. It is very simple to prepare and the hint of lemon makes it a refreshing dessert. Serve by itself or with a dollop of whipped cream and fresh berries.

1 cup butter, 2 sticks, room temperature

2½ cups powdered sugar, sifted before measuring

3 large eggs

Zest of one lemon

1¼ cups cake flour

1 teaspoon baking powder

½ teaspoon sea salt

⅓ cup cornmeal, fine grind

Additional powdered sugar

DID YOU KNOW?

Round, bright yellow and sweetly fragrant lemons contain the most juice, a potent zest, and a high concentration of vitamin C.

HELPING HANDS

Young children can help measure the cornmeal. Older ones can make the cake with supervision.

Preheat oven to 350°F. Butter and flour a 10 x 4-inch loaf pan.

Beat butter in a large bowl with an electric mixer for several minutes until fluffy. Slowly add the sugar. Beat for several minutes. Add eggs, one at a time, beating well after each addition. Beat in lemon zest.

Meanwhile, stir together flour, baking powder, salt, and cornmeal in a mixing bowl. Add to creamed butter and sugar. Mix on low speed until combined.

Pour batter into prepared pan and bake 50 to 60 minutes, or until a knife inserted into the center comes out clean.

Transfer cake to a rack to cool. With a knife, cut around pan sides to loosen it, then turn it out. Remove from pan and dust with powdered sugar.

VARIATIONS Mix in 1 cup melted, semisweet chocolate chips before adding the dry ingredients. The hint of lemon pairs nicely with the chocolate.

Double Chocolate Biscotti

PREP TIME: 20 MINUTES **COOK TIME:** 30 MINUTES **MAKES:** 30

This double-chocolate version of a traditional classic is a breakfast favorite of Claudia's husband, Greg. Enjoy with a cappuccino, at snack-time with milk, or for dessert with coffee.

FOR THE BISCOTTI:

1 cup almond meal (finely ground almonds)

2 cups all-purpose flour

½ cup sugar

½ cup brown sugar

1 teaspoon baking soda

½ teaspoon sea salt

½ cup cocoa powder

4 large eggs

¼ cup butter, melted

¼ cup Nutella, chocolate hazelnut spread

1 tablespoon pure vanilla extract

FOR THE FROSTING:

1 cup semisweet chocolate chips – melted separately

½ cup white chocolate chips – melted separately

Preheat oven to 350°F. Grease one baking sheet or line with a silicone baking mat.

Combine ground almonds, flour, sugar, brown sugar, baking soda, salt and cocoa in a large bowl. Mix well.

Put eggs in a large mixing bowl. Beat well. Add melted butter, Nutella and vanilla extract. Stir well or beat with an electric mixer. Stir in flour mixture. Dough will be stiff. Turn out onto prepared baking sheet, making two even rectangles of dough, measuring 10 x 3 x ½-inch.

Bake on the center rack for 20 to 25 minutes, or until a knife inserted near center comes out clean. Remove from oven and let cool for 5 minutes.

Starting from the narrow end and using a serrated knife, slice into ½-inch thick bars. Lay biscotti on their sides, on the same baking sheet. Put back in the oven and bake at 325°F. for 10 more minutes.

Remove and let cool for at least 30 minutes. Spread with a thin layer of melted semisweet chocolate and decorate with melted white chocolate. Allow chocolate to harden. Serve immediately or store in an airtight container.

Pour batter into prepared pan. Sprinkle with cinnamon sugar. Bake until top is light brown or until a knife inserted in the middle comes out clean, about 35 to 40 minutes. Remove from oven and let cool on a wire rack.

Dust with powdered sugar and cut into squares.

{ **VARIATIONS** Substitute one grated apple and I grated carrot for the pears. Bake in a muffin pan with paper liners. }

Limoncello Mousse

PREP TIME: 20 MINUTES   **CHILL TIME:** 2 HOURS   **SERVES:** 8

The mouth-puckering, zesty lemon flavor of this refreshing dessert is a welcome finish at any meal. Serving it with fruit is a good way to balance the rich taste of the whipping cream.

1 cup heavy whipping cream

½ cup sugar, divided

½ teaspoon plain gelatin

¼ cup Limoncello liqueur

4 large egg yolks, beaten

⅛ teaspoon sea salt

¼ teaspoon lemon zest, about one lemon

2 cups blueberries

CURIOSITY:

Blueberries are also called "brain berries" because of their anitoxidant and anti-inflammatory compounds.

KITCHEN TIP:

Young children and people in at-risk health groups should avoid eating foods that contain raw or lightly-cooked eggs.

Whip heavy cream until soft peaks form. Continue beating while slowly adding ¼ cup sugar until stiff peaks form. Refrigerate.

In the top of a double boiler, combine gelatin and Limoncello. Let soften for 5 minutes. Add egg yolks, ¼ cup sugar and salt. Beat over simmering water for 4 minutes.

Remove pan from simmering water and place in a large bowl filled with ice and continue beating for 4 minutes.

Fold whipped cream and lemon zest into lemon mixture. Divide into dessert dishes, add blueberries, and chill for several hours before serving.

VARIATIONS For an elegant presentation, layer the mousse alternately with fresh berries in tall parfait glasses. For a fun presentation, serve the mousse in hollowed-out lemons.

Black & White Semifreddo

PREP TIME: 60 MINUTES **FREEZER TIME:** 4 HOURS **SERVES:** 8

This semifrozen dessert, starring 3 layers of chocolate mousse, is similar to ice cream, yet easier to make. Its whipped goodness melts happily in your mouth.

DARK CHOCOLATE MOUSSE:

3 ounces semisweet chocolate

3 ounces bittersweet chocolate

2 tablespoons butter

4 large egg yolks

2 tablespoons sugar

½ cup heavy whipping cream

WHITE CHOCOLATE MOUSSE:

6 ounces white chocolate

1½ cups heavy whipping cream, divided

2 large egg yolks

2 tablespoons sugar

DARK CHOCOLATE MOUSSE *(makes 2 cups)*:
Combine both types of chocolate and butter in a small saucepan and place over low heat to melt, stirring constantly. (Or melt in a glass bowl in the microwave on 50% power for 2 minutes.) When melted, remove from heat and let cool 15 minutes.

Beat egg yolks and sugar in a large bowl with an electric mixer until fluffy, about 5 minutes. Add cooled, melted chocolate and mix.

In a separate clean bowl, beat whipping cream until stiff peaks form. Do not overbeat – it will turn to butter! Fold into chocolate mixture until well combined. Cover with plastic wrap and refrigerate.

WHITE CHOCOLATE MOUSSE *(makes 3 cups)*:
Combine white chocolate and ½ cup heavy whipping cream in a small saucepan. Place over low heat to melt, stirring constantly. (Or melt in a glass bowl in the microwave on 50% power for 2 minutes.) When melted, remove from heat and let cool 15 minutes.

Beat egg yolks and sugar in a large bowl with an electric mixer until fluffy, about 5 minutes. Add cooled, melted white chocolate and mix.

In a separate bowl, beat whipping cream until stiff peaks form. Fold into white chocolate mixture until well combined.

Line a 4 x 10-inch loaf pan with plastic wrap.

Spread about 1½ cups of the dark chocolate mousse in the bottom of the pan. Carefully spread about 1½ cups of the white chocolate mousse on top of the dark chocolate layer. Gently stir the remaining dark chocolate mousse into the remaining white chocolate, creating a light chocolate mixture. Use this light chocolate mixture to make the final layer.

Cover with plastic wrap and freeze for 4 hours or overnight. To serve, un-mold from the pan, remove the plastic wrap, let sit 5 minutes and cut into ½-inch thick slices.

Strawberry Cake

PREP TIME: 10 MINUTES   **COOK TIME:** 20 MINUTES   **SERVES:** 12

This is a great cake recipe for the beginner cook! It is easy to make and versatile.
Use it as a base for other layered desserts such as parfaits and ice cream cakes.

FOR THE CAKE:

4 large eggs

2 cups sugar

1 cup milk

1 tablespoon pure vanilla extract

2 cups all-purpose flour

2 teaspoons baking powder

½ teaspoon sea salt

FOR THE FILLING:

3 pints strawberries, rinsed and drained

2 cups heavy whipping cream

4 tablespoons powdered sugar, divided

FOR THE GARNISH:

Powdered sugar

Dark chocolate curls

Preheat oven to 350°F. Grease and flour three 8 or 9-inch round cake pans.

Beat eggs and sugar in a large bowl with an electric mixer until light and fluffy, about 7 minutes.

Heat milk and vanilla in a small saucepan over low heat to just scalding, or in a glass measuring cup in the microwave for 1 minute on high.

Stir together flour, baking powder and salt in a medium bowl.

When eggs and sugar are fluffy, add half the flour mixture and stir gently. Add ½ cup hot milk, stir to combine. Repeat with remaining half of flour mixture and ½ cup milk. Do not overmix! Pour batter into prepared pans.

Bake cake for 20 minutes, or until a tester inserted in the center of the cake comes out clean. Allow cake to cool completely before turning it out.

ASSEMBLE THE CAKE:
Remove tops from strawberries and slice thinly. Toss strawberries with 2 tablespoons powdered sugar, set aside.

Beat heavy whipping cream with 2 tablespoons powdered sugar until stiff peaks form.

Place one cake layer on a serving plate. Top with one-third of the whipped cream and about one-third of the strawberries – making an even layer. Repeat with remaining layers. You may not need to use all of the strawberries.

Garnish with powdered sugar and/or dark chocolate curls. Slice gently with a serrated knife and carefully serve each piece.

leftover inspirations

WITH A DASH OF IMAGINATION and a pinch of inspiration, leftovers can be transformed into great meals. Some of these dishes are so tasty that you will want to have leftovers just to make them! Begin with one leftover ingredient and start creating your own masterpiece.

Chicken Croquettes

About 2 cups cooked chicken, chopped in small pieces; 2 large potatoes, boiled and mashed; I cup cooked peas; I sprig fresh rosemary, finely chopped; 3 tablespoons finely chopped onion; ½ teaspoon sea salt; dash pepper; 2 eggs beaten; ¼ cup breadcrumbs; 2 cups canola oil for frying.

In a large bowl, mix chicken, mashed potatoes, peas, rosemary and onions. Roll into small balls. Dip balls into the beaten eggs, then roll in breadcrumbs and fry them in hot canola oil until light brown. Remove with a slotted spoon to a plate covered with a paper towel.

Chicken Salad

About 2 cups cooked chicken, chopped in small pieces; ½ cup bite-size apple chunks; ½ cup chopped celery; ½ cup halved grapes; I tablespoon slivered almonds; I tablespoon chopped green onion; ¼ cup mayonnaise; ½ teaspoon sea salt; dash pepper; dash curry powder, optional.

In a medium bowl, mix all ingredients. Keep cold.

Fajitas

About 2 cups cooked chicken (or steak) cut into bite-size pieces; 2 tablespoons olive oil; 4 onions; I bell pepper. MARINADE: I tablespoon worcestershire sauce; I can beer; I tablespoon cilantro, minced; juice of one lime; I tablespoon olive oil; I garlic clove, peeled and minced.

Combine marinade ingredients in a medium bowl. Add chicken and let sit for 20 minutes. Meanwhile, thinly slice onions and bell pepper, and sauté in olive oil for 10 minutes over medium heat. Drain the chicken and sauté in a few tablespoons olive oil for a few minutes. Add the cooked onions and peppers, and cook for a few more minutes. Serve on flour or corn tortillas – garnish with sour cream, guacamole and/or salsa.

Buonissima Salad, pg 80
Bella Salad, pg 72
Chopped Chicken Salad, pg 70
Grilled Chicken Ciabatta, pg 52
Pam's Chicken & Rice Soup, pg 235

Focaccia:

Croutons

Cut focaccia into ½-inch cubes and place on a baking sheet. Drizzle with olive oil and garlic salt. Mix well and toast in a preheated 350°F oven for 10 to 15 minutes.

Chips

Cut focaccia into ¼-inch slivers and place on a baking sheet. Drizzle with olive oil and bake in a preheated 350°F oven for 10 to 15 minutes.

Beef:
ground and cooked

Meatballs

About 2 cups ground meat; I garlic clove, peeled and minced; I tablespoon flat-leaf parsley; I egg; I boiled potato, mashed; ½ cup grated Parmesan cheese; I 15-oz can tomato sauce; ½-teaspoon salt.

Combine all ingredients – except the tomato sauce – in a medium bowl. Roll into small balls, and cook in a large nonstick skillet with 2 tablespoons olive oil for 5 minutes, shaking the pan often. Add tomato sauce and cook for 10 more minutes. Taste and adjust for salt and pepper. Serve with spaghetti.

Messy Meat Pie

About 2 cups cooked ground meat; I cup cooked sausage meat; I onion, peeled and chopped fine; 2 tablespoons butter; 2 tablespoons brandy; I tablespoon Italian seasoning; 2 large eggs; 2 slices of bread, soaked in a little milk then squeezed; ¼ teaspoon sea salt and dash pepper; two 9-inch ready-made pie crusts.

In a large skillet, sauté onion in butter. Add meats, brandy and Italian seasoning and cook until liquid has evaporated. Remove from heat, add eggs, bread, salt and pepper. Line a pie pan with one pie crust, fill with meat mixture, cover with second layer of dough. Seal sides. Brush top with a beaten egg. Cook for 45 minutes at 350°F.

Nachos

About 1 cup cooked ground meat; 1 large bag tortilla chips; 1 15-oz can refried beans; 2 cups grated cheddar cheese.

Place chips on a large plate, sprinkle with ground meat, dot with beans and cover with cheese. Microwave for 2 minutes. Garnish with salsa, chopped guacamole, sour cream and/or green chilies.

Steak: Exotic Steak Salad

4 to 8 ounces steak; ¼ fresh pineapple; 1 avocado; 1 tomato; ¼ cantaloupe; 2 tablespoons finely chopped onion; 4 cups mixed salad greens. DRESSING: ¼ cup olive oil; juice and zest of 1 lemon; 1 teaspoon curry and ¼ teaspoon sea salt.

Cut steak and salad ingredients and mix in a large bowl with salad greens. Whisk together dressing ingredients and toss with salad.

Tri-tip Panino, pg 58
Tri-tip Salad, pg 88

Egg Whites: Meringues

Preheat the oven to 200°F. Line 2 baking sheets with parchment paper or silicone baking mats. Place 2 egg whites and ¼ teaspoon cream of tartar in a large mixing bowl. Whip with electric beaters until soft peaks form. Beat in ½ cup sugar, one tablespoon at a time. Continue beating until egg whites are glossy and hold a stiff peak. Drop by spoonfuls onto lined baking sheets, leaving 1 inch of space between cookies. Place in preheated oven and bake for 2 hours. Turn off oven and leave the cookies (undisturbed) in the oven for at least 4 hours or overnight. Makes 12.

Fritatta:

Panino

Place a slice of frittata between 2 pieces of bread. Add thinly sliced fresh tomatoes and/or lettuce.

Pasta:

"Torta" or "Frittata"

Never throw away leftover pasta. Just mix with 2 beaten eggs, some grated Parmesan cheese, a little sea salt and pepper. Grease a 9-inch pie pan and bake in a preheated 325°F oven for 20 minutes to make a torta, or cook in a nonstick skillet to make a frittata.

Polenta:

Fried

Cut polenta in slices and fry in a skillet with butter and fresh sage.

Baked Polenta with Cheese

Polenta; I cup blue cheese crumbles, fontina or grated mozzarella (or cheese you have on hand.) I cup grated Parmesan cheese;

Butter a 9 x 9-inch baking pan. Cut the polenta in slices and place in the pan. Top with a layer of cheeses, then another layer of polenta and finally a sprinkle of grated Parmesan cheese. Bake for 20 minutes.

Rice:

Cheese Torta

About 2 cups cooked rice; 2 ounces chopped ham; 2 eggs, beaten; 8 ounces grated mozzarella; ½ cup grated Parmesan cheese; dash sea salt and pepper.

Mix all ingredients together in a medium bowl. Pour into a buttered 9-inch pie dish. Bake in a preheated 325°F oven for 30 to 40 minutes, or until done.

Spinach Torta

About 2 cups cooked rice; 4 ounces boiled spinach, drained and squeezed; 2 eggs, beaten; 8 ounces grated mozzarella; ½ cup grated Parmesan cheese; dash sea salt and pepper.

Mix all ingredients together in a medium bowl. Pour into a buttered 9-inch pie dish. Bake in a preheated 325°F oven for 30 to 40 minutes, or until done.

Pam's Chicken & Rice Soup

About 1 cup cooked chicken, shredded; 1 cup cooked rice; ½ onion, peeled; 1 large carrot, peeled and cut in large pieces; 1 celery rib, rinsed and cut in large pieces; 5 cups chicken broth; ½ cup heavy cream; salt and pepper.

In a food processor, mince the onion, carrot and celery. In a medium saucepan, sauté minced vegetables in 2 tablespoons butter for about 5 minutes. Add chicken broth, bring to a gentle boil, reduce heat, cover and let simmer for 20 minutes. Remove from heat, add shredded chicken, cooked rice, cream and stir. Taste and adjust for salt and pepper.

Arancini

About 2 cups cooked rice or risotto; 8 ounces mozzarella cut in small cubes; 2 eggs, beaten; breadcrumbs; canola oil for frying.

Make a small ball of rice, push a piece of cheese into the center. Dip into beaten egg then roll in breadcrumbs. Fry in hot oil, about 5 minutes. Drain on a paper towel. Or place on a baking sheet, drizzle with ¼ cup olive oil and bake in a preheated oven at 350°F for 10 minutes. Serve immediately.

Artichoke & Rice Torta, pg 53

Seafood: Seafood Spaghetti

About 2 cups cooked seafood cut into bite-size pieces; ½ cup olive oil; 2 garlic cloves, peeled and chopped; 2 tablespoon chopped flat-leaf parsley; ¼ teaspoon red pepper flakes; 1 pound spaghetti.

In a large pan, sauté the garlic, hot pepper and parsley in the olive oil. Add fish and sauté for 2 minutes. Boil the pasta, according to package directions. Drain. Toss with sauce. Serve immediately.

Tomato Meat Ragu: Portobello Mushrooms

4 large Portobello caps, wiped clean with a damp towel; 2 tablespoons olive oil; 2 tablespoons balsamic vinegar; 2 tablespoons chicken broth; salt and pepper. 1 cup Tomato Meat Ragu, pg 96; 2 ounces Asiago cheese, grated.

Preheat oven to 350°F. Place mushroom caps in a 9 x 13-inch glass baking pan, gills up. Mix olive oil, vinegar and chicken broth in a small bowl. Pour evenly over mushroom caps. Sprinkle lightly with salt and pepper. Bake 20 minutes, covered with aluminum foil. Remove from oven. Divide Tomato Meat Ragu evenly over baked mushrooms. Top with cheese and return to oven until cheese melts.

Simple Tomato Sauce: Farfalle Portofino

1 pound butterfly (bowtie) pasta; 2 cups Simple Tomato Sauce, pg 110; ½ cup pesto, pg 120; 3 tablespoons olive oil; ½ cup grated Parmesan cheese.

Warm tomato sauce in a large serving bowl. Add the pesto and olive oil and mix well. Cook pasta according to package directions, drain and toss with the tomato-pesto sauce. Garnish with Parmesan cheese and serve immediately.

Vegetables: Creamy Vegetable Soup

About 2 cups cooked vegetables (such as carrots, butternut squash, spinach, asparagus, potatoes); I leek, rinsed well and finely chopped; 2 tablespoons olive oil; I cup chicken broth; dash sea salt and pepper; 2 tablespoons butter.

In a large skillet, sauté leeks in olive oil for 5 minutes. Add cooked vegetables, salt and pepper and sauté for 10 minutes. Add a little chicken broth and blend until smooth, adding chicken broth as necessary. Reheat. Taste and adjust for salt and pepper. Stir in butter.

Vegetable "Sformato"
(almost a quiche and not quite a frittata)

Use any variety of leftover vegetables. Here is an example using asparagus:

About 2 cups steamed asparagus, chopped fine; 2 potatoes, peeled, boiled and chopped fine; I leek or onion, chopped fine; 2 tablespoons olive oil, I½ tablespoons flour; 2 tablespoons butter; 2 cups chicken broth; 2 eggs, separated; ½ cup grated Parmesan cheese; ½ teaspoon sea salt; dash ground pepper.

Butter a 9 x 9-inch baking dish and dust with ⅛ cup breadcrumbs. Make a small batch of Béchamel with the flour, butter and broth. (Follow directions for Béchamel White Sauce on pg 97). Meanwhile, sauté leeks in olive oil for 10 minutes. Add cooked asparagus and potatoes. Stir. When the Béchamel is ready, stir in the sautéed vegetables, egg yolks and cheese. Beat egg whites until stiff peaks form. Gently fold into vegetable mixture. Pour into prepared baking dish. Bake in a preheated 350°F oven for 40 minutes.

Zucchini Frittata, pg 54

What Can I Cook with What I Have at Home

Change the everyday question "What SHOULD I make for dinner?" into "What CAN I make for dinner?" Check out your pantry for inspiration to create a tasty meal or a family favorite. Start with one ingredient, add a couple more, and dinner will soon be done.

IF I HAVE...	I CAN MAKE...
Almonds:	Almond Baked Halibut, 145
	Chicken Salad, 231
	Double Chocolate Biscotti, 216
	Florentines, 220
Anchovies:	Caesar Salad, 82
	Fusilli all Checca, 106
Apples:	Chicken Salad, 231
	Fruit Salad, 202
	Harvest Apple Crisp, 208
Artichokes:	Rice & Artichoke Torta, 53
Arugula:	Scampi e Fagioli, 76
	Tagliata, 172
Asiago:	Baked Gnocchi, 117
	Cheese Torta, 234
	Rice & Artichoke Torta, 53
	Portobello Mushrooms, 236
Asparagus:	Bella Salad, 72
	Creamy Vegetable Soup, 237
	Penne with Asparagus, 132
	Roasted Asparagus, 188
	Vegetable Sformato, 237
Avocado:	Avocado, Carrot, Potato & Green Beans, 84
	Buonissima Salad, 80
Barley:	Barley with Shrimp & Scallops, 102
Basil:	Avocado, Carrot, Potato & Green Beans, 84
	Barley with Shrimp & Scallops, 102
	Bella Salad, 72
	Bruschetta, 48
	Caprese Salad, 68

IF I HAVE...	I CAN MAKE...
	Creamy Tomato Soup, 86
	Eggplant Parmigiana, 192
	Farfalle Caprese, 134
	Farfalle Portofino, 236
	Fusilli alla Checca, 106
	Mozzarella & Tomato Focaccia, 52
	Orecchiette with Broccoli & Sun-dried Tomato, 100
	Pesto, 120
	Salmon with Pesto, 152
	Simple Tomato Sauce, 110
	Spaghetti al Pesto, 120
Beans:	
Cannellini:	Bruschetta, 48
	Cannellini Beans with Sage, 196
	Pasta e Fagioli Soup, 64
	Scampi e Fagioli, 76
Béchamel White Sauce:	Lasagna, 94
	Penne al Forno, 126
	Potatoes Gratin, 183
	Vegetable Sformato, 237
Beef:	
Ground:	Meatballs, 232
	Messy Meat Pie, 232
	Tomato Meat Ragu, 96
	Nachos, 233
Eye of Round:	Arrosto, 140
	Fondue Chinoise, 156
Porterhouse:	Tagliata, 172
Shanks:	Ossobuco, 160
Steak:	Tri-tip Panino, 58
	Exotic Steak Salad, 233
	Tri-tip Salad, 88

Loin:	Arrosto, 140
	Brasato with Red Wine, 148
Tri-tip:	Grilled Tri-tip, 174
	Tri-tip Panino, 58
	Tri-tip Salad, 88
Bell Peppers:	Baked Vegetables, 184
	Garden Salad, 83
	Peperonata, 198
Blueberries:	Fruit Salad, 202
	Fresh Berry Tart, 42
	Ricotta Berry Cheesecake, 218
Blue Cheese:	Baked Polenta with Cheese, 234
	Buonissima Salad, 80
	Caramelized Cauliflower, 197
	Tri-tip Salad, 88
Bread:	Bruschetta, 48
	Grilled Chicken Ciabatta, 52
	Tri-tip Panino, 58
Broccoli:	Orecchiette with Broccoli & Sun-dried Tomato, 100
	Broccoli, 197
Brussels Sprouts:	Brussels Sprouts, 182
Butternut Squash:	Butternut Squash Soup, 66
	Creamy Vegetable Soup, 237
	Roast Chicken with Vegetables, 177
Cabbage:	Chopped Chicken Salad, 70
	Minestrone, 78
Capers:	Chicken Roman Style, 176
	Fusilli alla Checca, 106
	Lemon Chicken Piccata, 162
Carrots:	Avocado, Carrot, Potato & Green Beans, 84
	Brasato with Red Wine, 148
	Carrots by Rose, 180
	Creamy Tomato Soup, 86
	Creamy Vegetable Soup, 237
	Garden Salad, 83

	Minestrone, 78
	Ossobuco, 160
	Pam's Chicken & Rice Soup, 235
	Pasta e Fagioli Soup, 64
	Roast Chicken with Vegetables, 177
	Scallops with Marsala, 158
	Simple Tomato Sauce, 110
	Vegetable Sformato, 237
Cauliflower:	Caramelized Cauliflower, 197
	Creamy Vegetable Soup, 237
Celery:	Brasato with Red Wine, 148
	Chicken Salad, 231
	Creamy Tomato Soup, 86
	Minestrone, 78
	Pam's Chicken & Rice Soup, 235
	Pasta e Fagioli Soup, 64
	Roast Chicken with Vegetables, 177
	Scallops with Marsala, 158
	Simple Tomato Sauce, 110
Cheese:	
Asiago:	Baked Gnocchi, 117
	Cheese Torta, 234
	Rice & Artichoke Torta, 53
	Portobello Mushrooms, 236
Blue Cheese:	Baked Polenta with Cheese, 234
	Buonissima Salad, 80
	Caramelized Cauliflower, 197
	Tri-tip Salad, 88
Feta:	Chopped Chicken Salad, 70
	Mediterranean Salad, 36
	Tomato, Cucumber & Red Onion Salad, 62
Fontina:	Baked Gnocchi, 117
	Baked Polenta with Cheese, 234
	Baked Vegetables, 184
	Grilled Chicken Ciabatta, 52
Mascarpone:	Strawberry Tiramisu, 210
Mozzarella:	Baked Gnocchi, 117
	Baked Polenta with Cheese, 234
	Caprese Salad, 68
	Cheese Torta, 234
	Chicken Pizzaiola, 144
	Eggplant Parmigiana, 192

IF I HAVE...	I CAN MAKE...		IF I HAVE...	I CAN MAKE...
Fusilli:	alla Checca, 106		**Milk:**	Béchamel White Sauce, 97
				Creamed Spinach, 187
Green Beans:	Avocado, Carrot, Potato & Green Beans, 84			Fresh Berry Tart, 42
	Green Beans, 195			Mashed Potatoes, 199
				Strawberry Cake, 228
Halibut:	Almond Baked Halibut, 145		**Mozzarella Cheese:**	Baked Gnocchi, 117
Herbs:	Grilled Chicken with Herbs, 171			Baked Polenta with Cheese, 234
	Minestrone, 78			Caprese Salad, 68
				Cheese Torta, 234
Ice Cream:	Affogato al Caffé, 212			Chicken Pizzaiola, 144
				Eggplant Parmigiana, 192
Lamb:	Lamb Chops, 146			Farfalle Caprese, 134
	Lamb Chops Milanese, 150			Mozzarella & Tomato Focaccia, 52
	Leg of Lamb, 170			
			Mushrooms:	Portobello Mushrooms, 236
Lasagna:	Lasagna, 94			Sautéed Mushrooms, 194
				Veal with Sherry, 164
Leeks:	Almond Baked Halibut, 145			
	Creamy Vegetable Soup, 237		**Olives:**	Chicken Cacciatora, 142
	Minestrone, 78			
			Onions:	Lentils & Rice with Caramelized Red Onions, 122
Lemon:	Lemon Chicken Piccata, 162			Penne al Forno, 126
	Limoncello Mousse, 224			Tomato, Cucumber & Red Onion Salad, 62
Lentils:	Lentils & Rice with Caramelized Red Onions, 122			
			Orecchiette:	with Broccoli & Sun-dried Tomato, 100
Lettuce:			**Pancetta:**	Spaghetti Carbonara, 124
Iceberg:	Chopped Chicken Salad, 70			
			Parmesan Cheese:	Fettuccine Alfredo, 38
Romaine:	Caesar Salad, 82			
	Buonissima Salad, 80		**Pasta:**	Farfalle Caprese, 134
	Tri-tip Salad, 88			Farfalle Portofino, 236
				Fettuccine Alfredo, 38
Red or Green Leaf:	Garden Salad, 83			Fettuccine with Peas, 136
				Fusilli alla Checca, 106
Mesclun Mix: (Mixed Greens)	Bella Salad, 72			Lasagna, 94
	Mediterranean Salad, 36			Orecchiette with Broccoli & Sun-dried Tomato, 100
	Mixed Greens, 74			Pasta e Fagioli Soup, 64
				Penne al Forno, 126
Mascarpone Cheese:	Strawberry Tiramisu, 210			Penne Arrabiatta, 92
				Penne con Scampi, 112
Mesclun Mix: (Mixed Greens)	Bella Salad, 72			Penne with Asparagus, 132
	Mediterranean Salad, 36			Seafood Spaghetti, 236
	Mixed Greens, 74			Spaghetti al Pesto, 120

IF I HAVE...	I CAN MAKE...
Shrimp:	Penne con Scampi, 112
	Barley with Shrimp & Scallops, 102
	Scampi e Fagioli, 76
Sole:	Meunier, 175
Spaghetti:	al Pesto, 120
	al Ragu, 98
	Café Luna, 104
	Carbonara, 124
	with Clams, 130
	with Seafood, 236
	with Simple Tomato Sauce, 110
Spinach:	Chicken Pinwheels, 166
	Creamed, 187
	Creamy Vegetable Soup, 237
	Frittata, 55
	Torta, 50
	Torta with Rice, 235
Strawberries:	Cake, 228
	Fresh Berry Tart, 42
	Fruit Salad, 203
	Tiramisu, 210
Sun-dried Tomatoes:	Chicken Pinwheels, 166
	Mediterranean Salad, 36
	Risotto Cakes, 108
	Orecchiette with Broccoli & Sun-dried Tomatoes, 100
Tomatoes:	Baked Vegetables, 184
	Bruschetta, 48
	Caprese Salad, 68
	Farfalle Caprese, 134
	Fusilli alla Checca, 106
	Garden Salad, 83
	Scampi e Fagioli, 76
	Tomato, Cucumber & Red Onion Salad, 62
	Tri-tip Salad, 88
Tomato Sauce:	Chicken Cacciatora, 142
	Chicken Pizzaiola, 144
	Chicken Roman Style, 176
	Creamy Tomato Soup, 86
	Eggplant Parmigiana, 192

IF I HAVE...	I CAN MAKE...
	Farfalle Portofino, 236
	Minestrone, 78
	Penne Arrabbiata, 92
	Penne con Scampi, 112
	Simple Tomato Sauce, 110
	Spaghetti Café Luna, 104
	Tomato Meat Ragu, 96
Tomato Meat Ragu:	Lasagna, 94
	Portobello Mushrooms, 236
	Spaghetti al Ragu, 98
Veal: Cutlet or Scaloppine:	with Sherry, 164
	Pizzaiola, 144
	Milanese, 150
	Piccata, 162
Shanks:	Ossobuco, 160
Walnuts:	Mediterranean Salad, 36
Zucchini:	Baked Vegetables, 184
	Frittata, 54
	Minestrone, 78
	Sautéed Zucchini, 195
	Tri-tip Panino, 58

kitchen secrets for success

SOMETIMES a simple kitchen tip is the key ingredient that transforms a challenging recipe into an easy one. These helpful hints will make the beginner cook feel confident in the kitchen and proud of the delicious results.

Nonna's Secrets

In Italian, Nonna means grandmother. Her kitchen is a very special place, filled with delicious aromas of favorite comfort foods. Learning how to cook from grandmothers and family members is a unique gift that lasts a lifetime. Preserving the recipes for future generations is an essential responsibility that assures the continuity of traditions and culture.

Apples: A sliced apple placed on a plate gets eaten ten times faster than a whole one sitting in a fruit bowl!

Asparagus: To check for freshness, "snap" off the tough ends. The fresh asparagus will break about an inch away from the bottom.

Avocado: To ripen, place in a paper bag with an apple. Store at room temperature for a few days.

Béchamel White Sauce: To prevent milk from sticking to the bottom of the pot during heating, first rinse the pot with cold water, then without drying it, add the milk.

Beets: Since beets take a long time to cook, prepare them before you need them and store them in the refrigerator. Add to salads for extra flavor and nutrition. Cut off the tops, rinse well and steam for 30 minutes or until tender. Soak in cold water, then peel off the skins.

Biscotti: Biscotti make a nice hostess gift. Pack them in an air-tight container and decorate with a colorful ribbon.

Butter: If you do not have butter, you can make it yourself. Whip heavy cream at high speed with a couple of ice cubes. The fat will separate from the whey and make a ball of fresh butter.

Chard: Chard is two vegetables in one – the stalks are crunchy like celery but sweeter, and the leaves are cooked like spinach. Rinse well. Cut off the stalk and cut into 2-inch pieces. Cook them for 4 to 5 minutes with onions in olive oil. Then add the leaves, and cook for 2 minutes longer.

Cheeses: To preserve cheese, add a cube of sugar to its container. The sugar will absorb the moisture and keep the cheese fresher longer.

Dessert: To remove the cake from its mold after it has cooled off, warm it up for a couple of minutes.

Dirty Pots: If your pots have a bad smell, rub the inside with a handful of moist tea.

Endive: Before serving, remove the bitter inside leaves.

Fish: To keep fish from sticking to the bottom of a pan, place it on a layer of sliced lemons.

Flour Coating: When flouring small pieces of meat, poultry or fish, put them along with the flour and seasonings in a plastic bag. Close the top and shake well.

Lemons: Choose round, bright yellow and sweetly fragrant lemons to guarantee the most juice, a potent zest and a high concentration of vitamin C.

Meatballs: To keep them tender and moist, add mashed potato or cubed bread that has been soaked in milk to the meat mixture.

Nuts: Toasting nuts brings out more of their flavor. To toast, spread them evenly on a baking sheet and toast in a pre-heated 350°F for 8-10 minutes. Allow to cool and store in an airtight container.

Onions: To avoid crying while chopping onions, place a small piece of bread on the tip of the knife. To get rid of the smell of onion on your hands, wash your hands in cold water and rub with lemon juice, coffee grounds, salt or potato peels. Do not use hot water, it fixes the smell on your hands.

To get rid of onion breath, eat an apple or chew some fresh parsley, citrus peel, or roasted coffee beans.

Oranges: To get more juice out of oranges put them in warm water for a few minutes before squeezing.

Parsley: To keep parsley green and happy, add a piece of cork to the water.

Potatoes: Don't buy potatoes that are soft or have cuts, bruises or decay. If potatoes have any green spots, cut them off before cooking. They could taste bitter and in large amounts can be toxic. Put peeled potatoes in water to keep them from turning brown. Use them within 2 hours to prevent the loss of water-soluble vitamins.

Rice: To prevent the rice from boiling over, add a tablespoon of olive oil to the pot. To prevent rice from sticking together, add a few drops of lemon juice to the pot.

Roast: For best results, sear evenly on all sides before placing in oven.

Rosemary: Extra rosemary can be dried by hanging in a dry place. Use in roasted vegetable dishes, soups, or stews.

Salt: To prevent salt from sticking to itself in humid weather, add some grains of uncooked rice to the salt shaker. If soups or sauces are too salty, add a peeled potato. It will absorb the extra salt.

Sauté: For best results when sautéing, make sure the olive oil or butter is hot before adding the food to the pan. Otherwise, the food may stick or not sear properly.

Shellfish: Use your nose to determine if shellfish is edible. Bad fish will give off an unpleasant odor.

Spoons: Use wooden spoons to stir food. Metal ones can change the flavors.

Vegetables: Use a little water and high heat to steam vegetables. Since steam is hotter than boiling water, vegetables will cook faster.

Whipping Cream: Heavy cream or "whipping cream" must be very cold in order to whip into big, fluffy mounds. For best results, chill the cream, beaters and bowl for at least 2 hours. Start beating at low speed until the cream begins to thicken, then increase the speed until the cream makes a stiff peak when the beaters are lifted.

Whipping Egg Whites: Egg whites produce the most volume when whipped at room temperature. However, they separate best from the yolks when cold.

Zucchini: Avoid buying larger zucchini because they can be less flavorful and may be bitter.

Ingredient Storage

Artichokes: Store in a plastic bag, in the refrigerator. Use within a few days. Rinse before using.

Asparagus: Store in a plastic bag, in the refrigerator. Use within a few days.

Basil: To keep basil fresh, put the stems in a glass of warm water.

Beets: Store uncooked beets in a plastic bag in the refrigerator. Store cooked beets in a sealed container in the refrigerator for 3 to 5 days.

Broccoli: Store in a plastic bag, in the refrigerator. Use within 4 days.

Butternut Squash (and other winter squash): Store at room temperature.

Carrots: Store in a plastic bag, in the refrigerator. Best used within 7 days.

Cauliflower: Store tightly wrapped in plastic in the refrigerator for up to 5 days.

Celery: Store in a plastic bag, in the refrigerator.

Cherries: Store at room temperature for up to three days. Or store in a paper bag in the refrigerator for up to 10 days.

Coffee: Fresh coffee makes the best coffee. Buy it in small amounts. Store whole beans in an airtight container in the freezer, not the refrigerator. Store ground coffee in an airtight and lightproof container in a cool, dry, dark place. After a few days it will begin to lose its flavor due to the combined assault of moisture, air, light and heat.

Corn: Sweet corn loses sugar every day after it is picked. Use it quickly. Store in a plastic bag, in the refrigerator. Use within a few days.

Flat-leaf or Italian Parsley: Store in the refrigerator, with the stems in a glass of water covered with a plastic bag.

Garlic: Store whole garlic in a well-ventilated spot, outside of the refrigerator.

Herbs, dried: Store in airtight containers away from heat, light and moisture.

Leeks: Store in a plastic bag in the refrigerator. Best used within a few days.

Mushrooms: Store mushrooms in a paper bag inside a plastic bag, and they will keep for a week – though they will lose some moisture. Trim the ends off the stems and use the rest.

Lettuce: Rinse well before eating, and then spin dry. Store in a plastic bag in the refrigerator for up to 2 or 3 days.

Melons: Store whole melons at room temperature and cut ones in the refrigerator.

New Potatoes: Store in a plastic bag in the refrigerator.

Olive Oil: Store in a cool, dry dark place in a glass, porcelain, or stainless steel container with a tight fitting lid. Do not store in plastic or reactive metals.

Onions: Store whole onions in a cool, dark place. Do not store them near potatoes, which give off moisture as well as ethylene gas, which can cause onions to spoil quickly. Cut onions should be wrapped tightly in plastic, refrigerated and used within two days.

Oranges: Store in the refrigerator. Fresh juice may turn bitter after a few days, so squeeze it fresh and drink it quickly.

Parmesan Cheese: Fresh Parmesan cheese keeps well in the refrigerator, if wrapped tightly in plastic wrap. Grated Parmesan cheese can be stored for longer periods in an airtight container in the refrigerator or freezer.

Peas: Most peas should be served the day of purchase because most varieties perish quickly. If refrigerated, they should be kept in a plastic bag. All fresh peas should be washed before they are cooked, but not before they are placed in the refrigerator.

Peppers: Store in a plastic bag in the refrigerator. Peppers will shrivel if stored for more than 4 days, except when cut and kept in water. Green bell peppers will stay fresh a little longer than the yellow and red ones.

Pine Nuts: Pine nuts come from pine trees. They have a high fat content and should be stored in an airtight container in the freezer.

Portobello Mushrooms: Remove the mushrooms from any wrapping and transfer to a tray or plate. Cover with dry paper towel. Store in the refrigerator. They should keep about 5 to 6 days.

Potatoes: Store in a cool, dark place. Do not store potatoes in the refrigerator, as the low temperature will cause the starch to turn to sugar which will cause them to darken when cooked.

Spices: Store in airtight containers away from heat, light and moisture.

Strawberries: Store in a paper bag in the refrigerator, use within a few days. Better yet, rinse then drain and leave in a bowl on the kitchen counter so everyone can eat them.

Tea: Store crushed or whole leaves in an airtight and lightproof container in a cool, dry, dark place. Just like coffee, its enemies are moisture, air, light and heat.

Tomatoes: Store whole, ripe tomatoes in a cool place – around 55°F. Do not store them in the refrigerator. Temperatures below 50°F can destroy that great tomato flavor and texture.

Store unripe tomatoes in a brown paper bag and leave them for a few days at room temperature to ripen. Store cut tomatoes in the refrigerator and use as soon as possible.

Zucchini: Zucchini are perishable, so buy only as many as you need. Store in a plastic bag in the refrigerator.

Ingredient Preparation

Apples: Put peeled apples in water that has been mixed with a few drops of lemon juice and a dash of salt to keep them from turning brown.

Artichokes: To cook, place in a pot with a few inches of boiling water. Steam until the lower leaves can be pulled from the choke, about 30 to 45 minutes.

Asparagus: Steam whole with the tips out of the water. Do not overcook.

Beans: When cooking dried beans, soak them overnight in plenty of water. Always throw away the first batch of cooking water, then add a tablespoon of oil to the second one. They will be easier to digest.

Carrots: Put peeled carrots in water to prevent them from turning brown.

Corn on the Cob: To cook, boil water, add the corn then remove it as soon as the water returns to a boil. (Corn that is not very fresh may take a few minutes longer.)

Hard Boiled Eggs: Place them in a saucepan with enough cold water to cover completely by 1 inch. Bring to a gentle boil over high heat. Reduce heat to medium and cook an additional 10 minutes. Immediately place eggs in ice water to help yolks stay bright yellow.

Leeks: Leeks are grown in sandy soil and need to be thoroughly rinsed. Cut off the outer leaves and trim the bottom. Rinse well. Begin cutting from the bottom, as you get closer to the green part, make sure to rinse away any dirt. You can also cut the stalk open and separate the leaves to make them easier to rinse.

Meat: To tenderize tough cuts of meat, soak it for a couple of hours in lemon juice or vinegar.

Mushrooms: With meaty mushrooms it's always a good idea to add water or broth while cooking, rather than additional oil.

Potatoes: Boiled potatoes should be started in cold water rather than hot, to guarantee even cooking from outside to inside during the long cooking time.

Spinach: Rinse several times under running water, or soak it in a bowl, as the crumpled leaves have a tendency to resist washing. Lift the leaves out of the soaking bowl, empty the water, and repeat.

Strawberries: To prevent strawberries from filling with water, rinse first and then remove stems.

Vegetables: Steaming is one of the best ways to cook vegetables. It helps maintain more of the vegetable's natural taste, texture and color. In a large pot, bring an inch or two of water to a boil over high heat.

Add vegetables, cover and steam for 2 to 3 minutes. (Potatoes take 15 to 30 minutes.)

Zucchini: Rinse them, pat them dry, and trim off the ends before cooking. Small zucchini can be sliced or cubed for cooking, larger ones can be sliced lengthwise, and the seeds removed.

Measuring Tips

When following a recipe, it is important to measure ingredients properly.

Dry measuring cups have an even rim; liquid measuring cups have a spout.

Measuring dry ingredients: Use dry measuring cups which are graduated in size from ¼ cup to 1 cup. Spoon the dry ingredient into the cup. Level off the top with the back of a butter knife or straight-edge spatula.

Use measuring spoons which are graduated from ⅛ to 1 teaspoon. Carefully pour the dry ingredient into the spoon. Level off the top with the back of a butter knife or straight-edge spatula. Even though the amount may be small, for best results, measure baking soda, baking powder, cream of tartar, salt, spices and yeast exactly.

Measuring liquid ingredients: Use liquid measuring cups — glass or plastic with graduated markings on the side, usually ranging from 1 cup to 4 cups in size. Place the cup on a flat, level surface. Pour the desired amount of liquid into the cup. Read the markings at eye level to guarantee an exact measurement.

Glossary

A

Active dry yeast: a leavening agent that produces carbon dioxide which causes dough to rise.

Al dente: literally "to the tooth" refers to the degree of doneness for pasta or risotto when it is cooked properly. When cut in half, you should see a tiny white dot.

All-purpose flour: a finely ground wheat flour good for most uses.

Arborio: a variety of Italian short grain rice used to make risotto.

Arugula: a type of lettuce with a sharp flavor, used mainly in salads.

Asiago: a relatively mild Italian cheese made from cow's milk.

B

Baking sheets: flat sheets of regular or nonstick aluminum, with a raised rim all around or just on one edge.

Balsamic vinegar: aromatic Italian vinegar made from reduced grape juice, aged and blended for many years.

Beat: to mix thoroughly with a spoon, whisk or beaters until well-combined and very smooth.

Blue cheese: blue-veined cheeses of many varieties with rich, tangy flavor and creamy to crumbly consistency.

Braise: to brown meat or vegetables in butter and/or oil, then cook them in a small amount of cooking liquid at low heat for a long period of time. This cooking process tenderizes the food by breaking down tough fibers and creates a full-flavored dish.

Broil: to brown the top of food by placing directly underneath a source of heat.

Broth: a flavorful liquid prepared by simmering meat, poultry, fish or vegetables in water with some added herbs. Home cooks tend to use the term broth where restaurant professionals use the word stock.

Bundt pan: decorative, nonstick pan with fluted sides and a tube to conduct heat to the center of the cake for more even baking.

Butterfly: to cut open a thick piece of meat or chicken. To butterfly a piece of meat, cut into it horizontally at the thickest part. Cut into the meat until you have nearly cut it in half so you can open it like you would a book.

C

Cannellini bean: a large white Italian kidney bean.

Capers: pickled flower buds from a Mediterranean plant.

Caramelize: to cause natural sugars in foods to become browned and flavorful while cooking over low to medium heat for a long period of time.

Chicken breast fillet: a tender piece of boneless chicken breast that has been cut horizontally at the thickest part.

Colander: cooking utensil with many holes, used for washing or draining all kinds of vegetables and fruits, beans, or pasta, and for straining solids from stock.

Core: to remove seeds and center from fruit.

Cream of tartar: a fine white powder added to egg whites before beating to improve stability and volume, or added to batter with baking soda to help baked goods rise.

Cut In: to work a solid fat, such as butter, into dry ingredients.

Cutlet: a thin, tender cut of meat.

D

Dash: a small amount – about $\frac{1}{16}$ teaspoon.

Deep fry: to fry foods quickly in a deep pot of very hot oil.

Deglaze: to lift caramelized drippings left in a pan after roasting or sautéing by adding liquid, such as dry white wine or broth, and stirring gently.

Degrease: to separate fat from liquid such as cooking juices or broth – performed using a spoon to skim fat from the surface, or by pouring into a degreasing cup that has a spout attached to the bottom.

Dice: to cut or chop food into small cubes.

Divided: refers to using some of an ingredient in one step, then the rest in a later step.

Double boiler: a double-pan system whereby one pot fits partway inside the other. The lower pot holds simmering water, which gently heats the mixture in the upper pot.

Dough hook: a mixer attachment used to mix and knead dough.

Dredge: to coat before cooking with dry ingredients such flour or breadcrumbs.

Drizzle: to slowly and evenly pour a liquid mixture in a fine stream over food.

Dust: to lightly coat a food with a powdery ingredient such as flour or confectioners' sugar, usually using a strainer.

E

Emulsify: to bind together liquid ingredients while whisking or blending vigorously.

F

Fillet: a tender piece of meat, poultry or seafood that has no bones.

Fold: to gently mix two or more ingredients together when you don't want them to deflate, such as with beaten egg whites or whipped cream. Cut down through the center of the batters with a rubber spatula, move across the bottom of the bowl toward the side, and gently move the spatula to the top. Continue, turning the bowl slightly each time until combined.

Fry: to cook and brown food in a specified amount fat, usually done very quickly so that a minimal amount of the fat is absorbed into the food.

Fontina: a type of semisoft Italian cheese with a mild and slightly nutty flavor.

Frittata: a cooked mixture of eggs and vegetables that resembles a thick omelette.

G

Garnish: to decorate a dish for presentation before serving.

Gelatin: a water-soluble protein that is dissolved in warm liquid, then chilled to become firm.

Grate: to pass foods such as cheeses, vegetables, citrus skins, spices or chocolate, against a grater.

Gravy moat or indentation: a depression around the edge of a cutting board that catches juices from meats.

Gremolata: an Italian garnish consisting of minced garlic, parsley, lemon rind, and sometimes shredded basil. It is most often used in garnishing Ossobuco.

Grill: to cook foods over high, direct heat.

Grind: to process foods finely in a grinder or processor.

Gratin: a dish topped with breadcrumbs and/or grated cheese, cooked first in the oven then finished under the broiler until golden brown.

J

Jellyroll fashion: rolling a base and a filling so that when cut, a pinwheel design is produced.

Julienne: to slice foods in matchstick-sized piece, about $\frac{1}{8}$-inch wide and 2-inches long.

L

Ladyfinger: a long and narrow sponge cake cookie that is used in various dessert recipes like tiramisu.

Leek: a vegetable that resembles a very large scallion, used mainly in soups and stews.

M

Mandoline: a very sharp, stainless steel kitchen utensil used for slicing vegetables into ultra thin slices.

Marinate: to add liquid ingredients to food in order to enhance flavor and/or tenderize after it sets for a given amount of time.

Mince: to cut into very fine pieces.

Mix: to combine ingredients with a spoon or beaters until well incorporated.

N

Non-reactive cookware: cooking utensils that will not react with the food they contain.

Nutmeg: a pungent and aromatic seed that when grated is used to flavor both desserts and savory dishes.

O

Olive oil: oil produced from ripe olives. The highest quality olive oil is extra-virgin, which comes from the very first press.

Oregano: an herb that originated in the Mediterranean and is widely used in a variety of Italian dishes.

P

Paddle attachment: an attachment to an electric mixer that is used for most mixing purposes.

Parchment: heat resistant paper that is used to line baking pans or to cook food in a "package."

Pat: to press gently on food with the palm of your hand in order to place dry ingredients on the surface, or in conjunction with a towel to remove excess moisture.

Preheat: to heat oven to the specified temperature before adding the food.

R

Reduce: to simmer liquids such as a sauce or gravy, in order to reduce the volume and concentrate the flavors.

Roast: to cook meat or vegetables in an open pan inside an oven at high heat.

Refresh: to restore by placing in water.

S

Saffron: the most expensive spice that is harvested from the purple crocus flower for its aromatic flavor.

Sauté: literally means "to jump." To cook food in a small amount of oil or butter over high heat for a short time. Sautéing is best suited for thinner cuts of meat, fish, veal and chicken breast, or meat cut into pieces or strips. All vegetables can be sautéed.

Sea salt: salt that is the result of the evaporation of sea water. Can be obtained in large-grain or fine crystals.

Sear: to cook meats quickly on all sides over high heat to improve appearance and intensify the flavor.

Shred: to cut, slice or tear into thin strips.

Simmer: to cook gently, just below the boiling point.

Skinless chicken breast fillet: a tender piece of skinless and boneless chicken breast that has been cut horizontally at the thickest part.

Steam: to cook foods in a very small amount of liquid, usually water, so the heat cooks the food while the vapors keep it moist.

Stir: to move foods around with a spoon in a circular motion. Stirring is done to move foods when cooking. It is also used to cool foods after cooking. Most importantly, if a recipes calls for stirring to combine foods, such as a batter, before cooking, it usually means to gently mix just until well combined, as opposed to beating, which takes more strokes.

Stiff peaks: refers to shape of whipped cream or egg whites when they achieve the required volume necessary for a recipe.

Strain: to remove solid particles by passing a liquid or moist mixture through a colander, sieve or cheese cloth.

Sun-dried tomatoes: dried tomatoes that are found dry or stored in olive oil.

T

Tent: to loosely cover meat with foil during the resting period so that it stays warm but does not attract too much moisture.

Thyme: an aromatic herb which is distinguished by its small green leaves and purple flowers.

Toss: to combine ingredients by gently mixing until well-coated.

Translucent: clear or see-through, usually refers to onions that are cooked over medium heat in butter or olive oil until they have a transparent appearance.

V

Vinaigrette: a mixture of oil and vinegar, usually seasoned with herbs and spices.

W

Whip: to beat briskly with a wire whisk or electric mixer to increase volume by incorporating air.

Whisk: a utensil with looped wires at the end used for mixing or blending ingredients into a smooth consistency.

Whisk: to beat rapidly until smooth, light and airy.

Whisk attachment: a mixer attachment used for whipping.

Worcestershire sauce: a flavorful combination of malt vinegar, molasses, sugar, shallot, garlic, tamarind, clove, anchovy essence and meat extract.

Z

Zest: the thin outer peel of a citrus fruit used for flavoring. To zest a lemon use a fine grater or zester.

Two Peas in a Pot

Rima and I were introduced because I speak Italian; we became friends because we are kindred spirits. Our common Italian heritage provides the foundation for a solid friendship which has blossomed over the years. Our differences provide balance – I am the baker and pasta maker, she is the front line chef. Our similarities complement each other – we both love feeding and nurturing others. We share a profound passion for cooking, a resolute work ethic and a commitment to improving the world in which we live. We laugh daily as we discover a new trait that we share, a mannerism unique to only us.

Someone once asked if we had ever argued, or worse, started throwing food at each other? The question surprised us – such a foreign concept to the reality of our friendship. After observing our shared passion for charity, shopping, and travel, her husband once commented that we are like "two peas in a pod."

You have to meet Rima to appreciate her compassion, candor and concern for others. Her zest for life cannot be captured by print alone. She inspires me and others by her devotion to her family and friends, and by her dedication to improving her local and global communities. Every day our partnership grows stronger, our friendship deeper – and, as Rima says, with her lovely Italian accent, "We are like 'two peas in a pot!'"

–Claudia Pruett

Who finds a friend, finds a treasure!

Claudia is one of the first people I met when I arrived in the United States. Mutual friends introduced us because we have "beautiful Italy" in common. With her determination and loving ways, she immediately won my respect and admiration. As I was getting to know her, I realized how effortlessly we understood each other. Claudia is a very caring, giving person. Nothing gives her more joy than pleasing the people around her, starting by her own family. The quality I love the most about Claudia is something she does not flaunt, but she has a lot of. It's her compassion. Quietly, she does all she can for the needy. Her favorite field is helping "lost girls" and she is great at it. Claudia takes a good amount of her own time and devotes it to those girls. She makes them feel loved, and an important part of her life. She gives them the hope that they need to have a chance to make it in life.

Claudia is a great business partner. Her work ethic is unwavering, always focused, organized and never too tired. She always keeps me challenged and interested. She is an even more wonderful friend. I know I can count on her in any situation, anywhere in the world. There is an Italian proverb that says: Who finds a friend, finds a treasure. I am one of the lucky ones. I have Claudia to count on, to help me make sure that our joint efforts will make a difference!

–Rima Barkett

Acknowledgments:

So many wonderful people helped us create this book. It is truly difficult to include everyone by name, but absolutely necessary that we acknowledge how much we appreciate their help, advice and support. Nothing is more valuable than sincere words of encouragement from those we love. From our families who always encouraged us to do what we enjoy and who never tired of testing recipes, to our many friends who helped out in a moment's notice, to professionals who gave their time and advice for our success — we thank, from the bottom of our hearts, everyone who helped us realize our dream.

Credits:

FOOD STYLIST — Irene Bertolucci, www.ifoodstylist.com
FOOD PROPS — Beyond Pots & Pans
BOOK DESIGN — Marianne Mitten, Mitten Design
PHOTOGRAPHER — Michael Collopy

A tavola together
Cooking for the Family Table

WEEK 1: MENU

Lemon Chicken Piccata, pg 162
Spaghetti al Pesto, pg 120
Sautéed Peas, pg 188

Salmon with Pesto, pg 152
Risotto, pg 108
Green Beans, pg 195

Grilled Chicken with Herbs, pg 171
Risotto Cakes, pg 109
Creamed Spinach, pg 187

Fettuccine with Peas, pg 136
Baked Vegetables, pg 184
Garden Salad, pg 83

Dessert of the week:
Chocolate Chip Cookies, pg 206

GROCERY LIST

Extra Items for Your Family: milk, eggs, bread, fruits, vegetables, etc.

_____
_____
_____
_____
_____
_____
_____
_____
_____
_____
_____
_____
_____
_____
_____
_____
_____
_____

COOKING DINNER Simple Italian Family Recipes Everyone Can Make

WEEK 2: MENU

Arrosto, pg 140
Penne Arrabbiata, pg 92
Cannellini Beans with Sage, pg 196

Lamb Chops, pg 146
Potatoes Gratin, pg 183
Tomato, Cucumber & Red Onion Salad,
    pg 62

Chicken Pizzaiola, pg 144
Spaghetti Café Luna, pg 104
Mixed Greens, pg 74

Eggplant Parmigiana, pg 192
Bruschetta, pg 48

Dessert of the week:
Ricotta Berry Cheesecake, pg 218

GROCERY LIST

Extra Items for Your Family: milk, eggs, bread, fruits, vegetables, etc.

_____
_____
_____
_____
_____
_____
_____
_____
_____
_____
_____
_____
_____
_____
_____
_____
_____
_____

COOKING DINNER Simple Italian Family Recipes Everyone Can Make

WEEKLY Ingredients

PRODUCE
- [ ] 2 large tomatoes for baking
- [ ] I bunch radishes
- [ ] I head green leaf lettuce
- [ ] 3 pounds fresh spinach or I pound frozen
- [ ] I bell pepper
- [ ] I small eggplant
- [ ] I pound fresh or frozen green beans
- [ ] I small summer squash
- [ ] I small zucchini squash
- [ ] I red onion
- [ ] 2 onions
- [ ] I bunch flat-leaf parsley
- [ ] 5 oz fresh basil
- [ ] 2 lemons

PANTRY
- [ ] 3 15-oz cans chicken broth
- [ ] I pound fettuccine

MEAT/POULTRY/FISH
- [ ] 3 pounds chicken breast: boneless, skinless fillets
- [ ] I pound salmon fillets

DAIRY
- [ ] 4 oz blue cheese crumbles
- [ ] 4 oz mozzarella or fontina cheese

MISCELLANEOUS
- [ ] 2 10-oz packages frozen peas
- [ ] I jar capers
- [ ] I oz pine nuts

PANTRY ESSENTIALS (to have on hand)

STAPLES
- [ ] balsamic vinegar
- [ ] extra-virgin olive oil
- [ ] olive oil
- [ ] sea salt, plain salt, pepper
- [ ] all-purpose flour
- [ ] Arborio rice
- [ ] kidney beans
- [ ] spaghetti

FRIDGE
- [ ] eggs
- [ ] milk
- [ ] butter
- [ ] heavy whipping cream
- [ ] Parmesan cheese, chunk and grated
- [ ] garlic cloves
- [ ] carrots
- [ ] breadcrumbs
- [ ] dry white wine
- [ ] sun-dried tomatoes, oil-packed

FRESH
- [ ] tomatoes

HERBS AND SPICES
- [ ] oregano, dried
- [ ] thyme, dried
- [ ] nutmeg, ground

ADDITIONAL
Ingredients for dessert
- [ ] sugar
- [ ] baking soda
- [ ] cream of tartar
- [ ] pure vanilla extract
- [ ] semisweet chocolate chips

WEEK I

WEEKLY Ingredients

PRODUCE
- [ ] 2 large tomatoes for salad
- [ ] 6 roma tomatoes
- [ ] 5 oz mixed greens
- [ ] 2 lemons
- [ ] 2 large eggplants
- [ ] I cucumber
- [ ] I red onion
- [ ] 2 bunches fresh basil
- [ ] I bunch fresh sage
- [ ] I bunch fresh mint
- [ ] 2 pounds potatoes

PANTRY
- [ ] 4 15-oz cans plain tomato sauce
- [ ] 2 15-oz cans cannellini beans
- [ ] I pound spaghetti

MEAT/POULTRY/FISH
- [ ] I 4 to 5 pound eye of round roast
- [ ] 8 4-oz lamb chops
- [ ] I pound chicken breast: boneless, skinless fillets

DAIRY
- [ ] 4 oz feta cheese, crumbled
- [ ] 3 8-oz balls fresh mozzarella
- [ ] ½ pint heavy whipping cream

MISCELLANEOUS
- [ ] I baguette

PANTRY ESSENTIALS (to have on hand)

STAPLES
- [ ] balsamic vinegar
- [ ] extra-virgin olive oil
- [ ] olive oil
- [ ] sea salt, plain salt, pepper
- [ ] canola oil or peanut oil for frying
- [ ] red wine vinegar
- [ ] all-purpose flour
- [ ] diced tomatoes, canned
- [ ] penne pasta
- [ ] chicken broth

FRIDGE
- [ ] eggs
- [ ] milk
- [ ] butter
- [ ] Parmesan cheese, chunk and grated
- [ ] onion
- [ ] garlic cloves

HERBS AND SPICES
- [ ] fresh rosemary
- [ ] red pepper flakes
- [ ] nutmeg, ground

ADDITIONAL
Ingredients for dessert
- [ ] sugar
- [ ] pure vanilla extract
- [ ] cornstarch
- [ ] 8 oz plain yogurt
- [ ] 16 oz ricotta cheese
- [ ] I pkg graham crackers
- [ ] I pint blueberries

WEEK 2

WEEK 3: MENU

Spaghetti al Ragu, pg 98
Spinach Frittata, pg 55
Focaccia, pg 32

Chicken Pinwheels, pg 166
Mashed Potatoes, pg 199
Carrots by Rose, pg 180

Lasagna, pg 94
Caprese Salad, pg 68

Farfalle Caprese, pg 134
Caesar Salad, pg 82

Dessert of the week:
Strawberry Tiramisu, pg 210

GROCERY LIST

Extra Items for Your Family: milk, eggs, bread, fruits, vegetables, etc.

COOKING DINNER Simple Italian Family Recipes Everyone Can Make

---

WEEK 4: MENU

Veal with Sherry, pg 164
White Rice, pg 137
Broccoli, pg 197

Penne con Scampi, pg 112
Garden Salad, pg 83

Spaghetti with Simple Tomato Sauce, pg 111
Peperonata, pg 198

Sea Bass in Parchment, pg 168
Basmati Rice, pg 137
Mixed Greens, pg 74

Dessert of the week:
Mocha Marble Cake, pg 204

GROCERY LIST

Extra Items for Your Family: milk, eggs, bread, fruits, vegetables, etc.

COOKING DINNER Simple Italian Family Recipes Everyone Can Make

WEEKLY Ingredients

PRODUCE
- ☐ 4 large tomatoes for salad
- ☐ 2 heads romaine lettuce
- ☐ 2 pounds carrots
- ☐ 3 pounds russet potatoes
- ☐ 2 onions
- ☐ I bunch fresh basil

PANTRY
- ☐ 2 15-oz cans plain tomato sauce
- ☐ I pound bowtie pasta
- ☐ I pound lasagna pasta

MEAT/POULTRY/FISH
- ☐ I pound lean ground beef
- ☐ I pound chicken breast: boneless, skinless fillets

DAIRY
- ☐ 2 8-oz balls fresh mozzarella
- ☐ I dozen fresh eggs

MISCELLANEOUS
- ☐ I bag croutons
- ☐ I 12-oz bottle club soda
- ☐ 2 10-oz pkgs frozen spinach, chopped

PANTRY ESSENTIALS *(to have on hand)*

STAPLES
- ☐ extra-virgin olive oil
- ☐ olive oil
- ☐ sea salt, plain salt, pepper
- ☐ all-purpose flour
- ☐ active dry yeast
- ☐ tomato paste
- ☐ spaghetti

FRIDGE
- ☐ eggs
- ☐ milk
- ☐ butter
- ☐ heavy whipping cream
- ☐ Parmesan cheese, chunk and grated
- ☐ mozzarella cheese
- ☐ garlic cloves
- ☐ Dijon mustard
- ☐ dry white wine
- ☐ anchovies

HERBS AND SPICES
- ☐ nutmeg, ground

ADDITIONAL
Ingredients for dessert
- ☐ sugar
- ☐ powdered sugar
- ☐ cognac
- ☐ I 12-oz pkg Italian ladyfinger cookies
- ☐ 16 oz mascarpone cheese
- ☐ 16 oz frozen strawberries
- ☐ I pint fresh strawberries

WEEKLY Ingredients

PRODUCE
- ☐ I head green leaf lettuce
- ☐ 5 oz mixed greens
- ☐ I bunch radishes
- ☐ 3 bell peppers, red, yellow, green
- ☐ I pound fresh broccoli
- ☐ I small zucchini squash
- ☐ 8 oz white mushrooms
- ☐ I bunch flat-leaf parsley
- ☐ I bunch fresh oregano
- ☐ I bunch fresh thyme

PANTRY
- ☐ I bottle dry sherry
- ☐ I bottle brandy
- ☐ I pound spaghetti
- ☐ I pound penne pasta

MEAT/POULTRY/FISH
- ☐ 1½ pounds sea bass fillets
- ☐ I pound medium prawns
- ☐ I pound veal scaloppine

DAIRY
- ☐ 4 oz blue cheese crumbles

PANTRY ESSENTIALS *(to have on hand)*

STAPLES
- ☐ balsamic vinegar
- ☐ extra-virgin olive oil
- ☐ olive oil
- ☐ sea salt, plain salt, pepper
- ☐ all-purpose flour
- ☐ long grain white rice
- ☐ basmati rice
- ☐ kidney beans
- ☐ plain tomato sauce
- ☐ diced tomatoes, canned
- ☐ parchment paper

FRIDGE
- ☐ eggs
- ☐ milk
- ☐ butter
- ☐ heavy whipping cream
- ☐ Parmesan cheese, chunk and grated
- ☐ onion
- ☐ garlic cloves
- ☐ carrots
- ☐ celery
- ☐ breadcrumbs

FRESH
- ☐ tomatoes
- ☐ potatoes
- ☐ lemon

HERBS AND SPICES
- ☐ red pepper flakes

ADDITIONAL
Ingredients for dessert
- ☐ sugar
- ☐ brown sugar
- ☐ powdered sugar
- ☐ baking soda
- ☐ baking powder
- ☐ coffee
- ☐ semisweet chocolate chips
- ☐ pure vanilla extract
- ☐ I cup sour cream